The Limits of Schooling

Peter Marin is primarily a writer and a poet. He attended the University of Wisconsin, Swarthmore College (B.A., 1955), Columbia University (M.A., 1958) and Brandeis University. Marin has taught and lectured at a number of colleges, including California State University, Los Angeles, and International Community College. Marin was director of Pacific High School in 1967–68 and a visiting fellow at the Center for the Study of Democratic Institutions in 1968–69. He has written extensively about education in a number of periodicals and is the co-author (with Allen Cohen) of *Understanding Drug Use* (1971) and the author of *In a Man's Time* (1974).

Vincent Stanley attended Pacific High School and was its assistant director in 1967–69. He later attended St. John's College, and in 1971 edited the *New Schools Exchange Newsletter* with Peter Marin. Stanley is a fiction writer and is currently employed as the sales manager of a mountain climbing equipment manufacturing company in Ventura, Calif.

Kathryn Marin was educated at Swarthmore College (B.A. 1955) and was trained in early childhood education through the Montessori program. In the 1960's she taught in the Head Start program in Los Angeles, and at both pre-school and elementary levels in Montessori schools. Marin edited the *New Schools Exchange Newsletter* from 1971–73.

PETER MARIN
VINCENT STANLEY
&
KATHRYN MARIN

The Limits of Schooling

Prentice-Hall, Inc.   Englewood Cliffs, N. J.
A SPECTRUM BOOK

Library of Congress Cataloging in Publication Data
Marin, Peter, comp.
　The limits of schooling.

　(A Spectrum Book)
　CONTENTS: Marin, P. Introduction.—Free schools and their roots: Dennison, G. From: The lives of children. Kozol, J. Free schools.—Deschooling: Goodman, P. The universal trap. Illich, I. The alternative to schooling. [etc.]
　1. Educational innovations—Addresses, essays, lectures.　2. Free schools—Addresses, essays, lectures.　I. Stanley, Vincent, joint comp.　II. Marin, Kathryn, joint comp.　III. Title.
LB1027.M3185　　　371　　　74–28374
ISBN 0-13-536938-X
ISBN 0-13-536920-7 pbk.

© 1975 by Prentice-Hall, Inc., Englewood Cliffs, New Jersey. A SPECTRUM BOOK. All rights reserved. No part of this book may be reproduced in any form or by any means without permission in writing from the publisher. Printed in the United States of America.

10　9　8　7　6　5　4　3　2　1

PRENTICE-HALL INTERNATIONAL, INC. (*London*)
PRENTICE-HALL OF AUSTRALIA PTY. LTD. (*Sydney*)
PRENTICE-HALL OF CANADA LTD. (*Toronto*)
PRENTICE-HALL OF INDIA PRIVATE LIMITED (*New Delhi*)
PRENTICE-HALL OF JAPAN, INC. (*Tokyo*)

Contents

Introduction   1
Peter Marin

PART ONE: Free Schools and Their Roots   15

From: THE LIVES OF CHILDREN   19
George Dennison

Free Schools   39
Jonathan Kozol

PART TWO: Deschooling   55

The Universal Trap   59
Paul Goodman

The Alternative to Schooling   69
Ivan Illich

PART THREE: Public School Reform: The Open Classroom   83

The Problem of Choice 87
John Holt

Beginning the School Year 105
Herbert Kohl

PART FOUR: Public Schools: Beyond Pedagogy 119

The Unlived Life 123
Sylvia Ashton-Warner

The Price of Amphibians 135
James Herndon

The Limits of Schooling

Introduction

The essays in this collection are not merely about schooling. They are also about freedom. In almost all of them pedagogical concern gives way to something larger, more significant: a desire not to "improve" the schools, but to move past them into the world, to replace them *with* the world. That is why the collection is called "the *limits* of schooling"—because these essays push against and past those limits, trying to break the hold which schooling exercises not only on the young but also on our adult imaginations. What is called into question here are the assumptions we make mindlessly and habitually about education without ever examining them. Without hesitation those assumptions are set aside, replaced by a more basic and sustaining concern: the world of unmanaged experience lying just beyond the institutional constraints we put upon it. What the writers of these essays share is a felt sense of life, an insistence on the primacy of experience, a love of the world—by which I mean, in this context, the raw stuff of life always at odds with the roles and rituals maintained in the schools. These writers reject not only the methods of the schools, but also their structure and function, their existence itself. They feel we would be better off without them, and even when the existence of schools is taken for granted, when the hope of doing away with them is set aside, no faith is put in them; they are simply understood as a permanent condition, a kind of weather, in which one does whatever is sensible, possible.

It is important to understand, in a general way, the reasoning behind that attitude. Though it varies from essay to essay, I would characterize it as a shared rejection of the institutionalization of experience, a reaction to the state's monopoly of the imagination, time and energy of the young, and an attempt to establish radical, communitarian alternatives to it. What is clear to all these writers is that the damaging effects of the schools are neither accidental nor incidental to their purposes; they understand them to be the inevitable and even intentional result of the aims of the schools. Though some do not say so explicitly, almost all of them see past the usual myths and rhetoric of schooling to what the schools really are: the underpinning of the nation-state, the American empire. That perception is what moves them in the directions they take, away from a belief in small changes and toward more sweeping criticisms and solutions, for they understand that the schools are designed to do precisely what they do: define a social and psychic reality for the young, reproduce it in and through them and diminish whatever volition, energy and imagination seem at odds with that reality.

In short, the schools serve the state, and since the state they serve is an empire, they do what the institutions of empire have always done: they substitute for localized, volitional and organic relation the coercive, authoritarian and hierarchial relations which form the skeletal structure of the institution itself. They exhibit the characteristics that Lewis Mumford insists are the main institutional processes of empire: standardization, mechanization and quantification. As in the early theocratic states like Egypt or Babylonia, or the great centralized modern states, those processes become in our schools the standards of efficiency against which all activity is measured. The schools monopolize and occupy time, energy, space and imagination, laying upon them an artificial grid of programming, scheduling, tracking and grading. Those primary sources, which belong ideally to the individual and community, which are in fact alive within them, become the institution's property and are doled out in bits and pieces, as if the institution itself was their source: both their custodian and creator. Thus, whatever their own intentions, teachers and administrators find themselves acting, always, through the skeletal *form* of the schools, and that form is the miniaturized form of empire, the idea of empire made small and frozen into role and ritual. Within that form, as in the organization of all empires, the organic relation of the individual to the world is broken; the young gradually cease to inhabit the world or sense its presence in themselves. They become, instead, encapsulated by the institution, attuned to it and defined by it, having no existence outside of the one it confers upon them.

That inner relation to empire is precisely what makes the schools so resistant to change; it is present in most attempts to change them. The solutions ordinarily offered for education crises are as lifeless and coercive as the system they are meant to change. They modernize the surface of schooling while leaving the deep structure of the schools intact. Though small changes make the schools more tolerable, more habitable for the young, they do nothing much to loosen the hold of schools upon energy and time, and the monopolization of experience remains unchallenged, as do the cultural attitudes behind it. One can see that most clearly in the language of "innovative" pedagogy: modular scheduling, accountability, behavior modification, problem-solving, feedback, classroom management . . . these are the terms of the factory and corporation. They are mechanical, lifeless, neither drawn from nor appropriate to organic or animal life, to a creaturely existence, but simply adapted to education from the world of the machine.

It is there, in that world view codified as speech, that one can perceive at work the attitudes which underlie both the schools and the changes suggested for them. Both areas reveal a poverty of imagination, a loss of felt existence. What disappears almost completely is any sense of what it might really mean to be free and self-directive, at home in the community or world. I do not mean by that simply the loss of vision or the dream of being free; I mean also the disappearance of the memory of what community and freedom have meant historically and philosophically. Those ideas are reduced in our traditional pedagogy to pat phrases and self-deceptive techniques. The closed sphere of the "open classroom" (which is indeed better than what it replaces) comes to stand in our fuddled minds for real freedom, space and choice; "individualized instruction" takes the place of relation; the "cognitive and affective domains" are mistaken for the full range of passionate and variable experience. The wide range of human possibility is everywhere trivialized, reduced to technique, to timidity masked as innovation, to control disguised as "help." The rich world dwindles and recedes; our diminished *idea* of the world takes its place. Slowly, as we adjust ourselves to that idea, we too dwindle, we lose sight of what it is we might have wanted, what it is we have lost or do not yet have.

The schools, of course, are not the only place in which that process occurs. They merely mirror what is going on simultaneously in many other realms: the political process, the media, even the ways we think, see and touch. The schools are simply the area in which we have ritualized it most completely and backed it most fully with the laws of the state. And one cannot even be quite sure whether or not the schools have been consciously designed to produce such a result, for it may simply be the inescapable consequence of something so deep in the culture that it enters our institutions beyond all choice. But whatever the case, it is clear that it is through the systematized destruction of relation and the slow diminishment of existence that the state intrudes itself so completely upon consciousness. To put it simply: in the relational void we create in the schools, the state takes the place of the world. The state not only surrounds the individual but also establishes itself inside, assumes a life within the individual that circumscribes thought in the same way that action has been circumscribed externally. It becomes a screen, a Chinese wall having the same function as the original wall: to keep the world out, to hold people in.

The effect of all this is a kind of sleep, what we can call a "sleep of empire": the loss of a sense of distance, openness, possibility. So far as pedagogy is concerned it means that the parameters of potential activity grow tighter and smaller, and instead of thinking about ways to help the young or making a larger place for them in the world, we go round and round thinking only about schools. There is, for instance, no graduate school in the country which offers a course in beginning or running a free school—or, for that matter, in envisioning alternatives of any kind to the massive system of schooling we have. Teachers are still trained everywhere to serve only the state and its schools. That is really no surprise, for teachers are trained in schools, and what can one expect from institutions of that sort save a dedication to their own continuity? They maintain themselves by inhibiting and limiting the imagination of those who pass through them, and the end result is a kind of massive crystallization, a loss of independence, so that it is the state itself which seems to see and speak through persons.

I remember being asked, a few years back, to address a group of San Francisco teachers about their problems with students and drugs. To introduce me, the superintendent of schools read from something I had written:

> Our schools are now expected to do what has traditionally been the task of the full community. We make them our churches, prisons, and foster homes; teachers become policemen and priests. It is there we hope to salvage civilization and the young—as if the schools were themselves a melting pot, a smelter, in which we can mix and blend and produce by sheer will a workable culture. The school's function becomes the structuring of ego, the control of behavior, the remaking of personality; wherever we face crises—racial, sexual, or political—we hope to resolve them in the schools.

When he had finished, he paused for a moment, looked at the audience feelingly, then said: "So you see, you and I have a big job to do, and Mr. Marin is here to help us do it."

It is that, precisely, that I mean. What the superintendent could not see was that I was protesting the schools' assumption of responsibility, was arguing that they had neither the expertise nor the right to assume that responsibility, and that the answers to such problems lay outside the ordinary activity of schools. In the paragraphs following the one he had read, I had gone on to say:

> But that won't work. Even when schools change, they change too slowly; we look at the young and believe we know what they need, and the machinery of education cranks and creaks into gear. But by the time the changes are complete, the young have changed again, and we are ready to handle a generation that has already disappeared. The distance between the world of the young and the schools steadily increases—and so does the damage the schools can do.
>
> The problem, put simply, is that schools have inherited and systemized what is worst in our community and history. What is elsewhere destruc-

tive but diffuse and rapidly dissolving is organized in the schools into curriculum and method. The corrosive role playing and demand systems are so extensive, so profound, that nothing really human shows through, and when it does, it appears only as frustration, exhaustion, and anger. The young are taught neither to be needed alive nor to be free, for one cannot be taught these things at all; they must be lived out in precisely those turbulent human relations the schools destroy. It is that, of course, which is their real outrage: the systematic corruption of the relations of adolescents to one another and adults. Where they should be comrades, allies, equals, and even lovers, the system makes them *teacher* and *student*—pawns in a thoughtless game of authority that reveals and changes nothing.

But he had not chosen to read those paragraphs, and I suspect that was not merely because they didn't serve his purposes, but because he also could not quite believe that I meant them. To do so would have called into question his role and the roles of the assembled teachers and the conference itself. Talking with the teachers it became quite clear that most of them identified themselves neither with the students nor their subjects nor even their own personal needs and affections; instead, they identified themselves with the schools, and any question raised about the schools was a question raised about them. Talking to them, one felt like one of those characters in a science-fiction film trying to warn his neighbors about the bugs from outer space and learning, with person after person, that they had already been possessed by them. The teachers too had been possessed, mesmerized. They were so occupied and preoccupied by the myth of the schools that they could not permit themselves to think seriously about the real nature of the schools, or alternatives to them.

That is where we are now, surrounded by that kind of sleep, still encapsulated in myth, and it brings us back to the importance and function of the essays collected here. Here and there these days one finds in educational thought a suggestion of real possibility, a crack in the usual walls. At the conference I have described there were a few teachers who had come on their own to believe in the necessity of a radical change in education. That is also the case elsewhere; people have begun to awake groggily from their entrancement. The essays in this collection testify to that fact. They present the particular trends and lines of thought that have shown up this past decade as part of what can be called "the radical education movement," and to understand them fully one must understand something about the movement behind them, the resistance to public schooling which has begun to develop during this past decade into several schools of thought.

Essentially, that movement has been an attempt to establish in one form or another alternatives to traditional schooling: areas of imagination and choice, cleared spaces in which both the young and old can begin to see or inhabit more fully what surrounds them. Sometimes, as in the free-school movement, that attempt has taken the participants out of the schools entirely, though not beyond the idea of schooling itself. At other times, perhaps more often, it has manifested itself in the insistence on "school reform": attempts to create within the schools small islands of choice protected as much as possible from the larger structure around them. And, finally, there has been the rapid growth of a third way of seeing things, one less practical and yet somehow more convincing, more liberating, an attempt to free both the young and the imagination itself: the idea of "deschooling," the belief that we ought to eliminate schools altogether, replace them with other ways of being with and educating the young.

Those three approaches are further complicated by the presence within them of two main traditions, often apparently at odds with one another. One tradition is what I would call an organic or existential tradition, and it is based fundamentally on a re-visioning of human nature. Its roots run down and back through the work of A. S. Neill and Paul Goodman to Wilhelm Reich and Freud and a few educators whose work has more to do with a kind of educational communalism than with pedagogy. It is essentially a "therapeutic" approach, though I use that word reluctantly, knowing no other, and meaning by it simply the belief that the right circumstances, as uncoercive as possible, can be used to allow and restore to the young their natural emotional and animal health. In this view, what lies at the heart of all individual and social health is a depth and freedom of experience: instinctual life, emotional freedom, sexual grace, independence, choice and a community of equals—all of which are taken as the necessary ground of any kind of decent learning.

The second line of thought, most fully expressed in what follows by the essays of Illich and Kozol, is far more political in content. As Kozol suggests, it runs in part back through the freedom schools established during the civil rights movement in the South, and it is also allied with the work of men like Paulo Freire, whose teaching of literacy is based on the idea of oppressed and "silent" cultures—those who have been deprived by institutions and the state of a language in which to describe the realities of their existence. In this view, the schools are seen as instruments of oppression, the means by which dominant races and classes maintain their power over others. The purpose of educational alternatives, whatever their nature, is to break the state's monopoly on knowledge, to liberate consciousness and to aid the disenfranchised in regaining the political power and participation they have been denied.

Taken together, these distinctions comprise the major trend of radical educational thought. Within the movement itself, there have been frequent internal disputes and schisms connected to these different ways of seeing things. Sometimes those disputes seem to be almost more important than the attitudes all share toward the public schools—if only because they seem to indicate fundamentally different attitudes about not only education, but also human nature, politics and values. I remember years ago attending a conference to which all of the "leading spokesmen" from the free-school movement had been invited. The differences I have mentioned surfaced there, and the conference was schismatic, turbulent. A few weeks later, in a piece written for a magazine, I wrote:

What emerged for me was a sense of the distances between various free school groups—in terms of how they define schools, childhood, and aspects of American reality. Some are primarily concerned with the hold institutions exercise on consciousness and experience, and with how educators of all sorts, radicals as well as reactionaries, are hemmed in by the limits of discourse they accept without question. We seem unable to discuss learning or survival unless we do it in terms of *schools*—and that indeed diminishes what we can say, imagine, and do.

On the edge of thought we have the notion of "deschooling," which is not so much a mode of activity as a thrust of reasoning and imagination. Those who accept the idea are at significant odds with those who see free schools as the only feasible alternative to state schooling. But even among the free school partisans there are divisions. Some seem committed to a Summerhillian, counterculture approach. Others see the Summerhillian method as escapist. They pay less attention to emotional and sexual changes than to questions of political potency and efficacy, and for them the struggle of the blacks and the poor is the central, usually the *only*, one. Though it might seem that these two approaches should coexist and feed each other, they are more often than not set against each other. This raises the question of whether, in fact, there really is a single free school "movement." What might be closer to the truth is that some persons are interested in alternative world views and life-styles, and others are interested in *political* change. Both groups, at the moment, are experimenting with "free" schools as a way of achieving change—but the allegiances on both sides are not really to new kinds of schooling but to *kinds of change*.

Beyond both these camps, of course, are the majority of people who are interested in improving our existing schools. In some ways this group draws ideas and inspiration from the free schools' doers and thinkers, even though these people usually feel that their ideas cannot be effectively transferred into the state's schools.

Sooner or later, in any discussion, these differences surface. The result is that there is no semblance of unanimity among those who believe in public schooling and no semblance of it among those who oppose public schooling. Both camps contain radically different views of the function of the state, the nature of learning, definitions of reality, society, the person—and the relations among them. Unfortunately, those views are rarely clarified. Were they expressed carefully and fully, the lines might not be drawn fuzzily, as they are now, between deschooling, free schooling, and public schooling. We might, instead, confront directly such issues as the relation between individual and state; the definitions of cultural and private value; our underlying historical direction; the nature of political reality and religious meaning; the relation of knowledge and experience. But because we are not accustomed to talking in clear detail about those issues, they are reduced (as in New Orleans) to fogged and meaningless arguments about *schooling*.

One sees, finally, that imagination has outstripped reality. Many of those who theorize about schooling have come to the end of the line and now speak only about deschooling. They realize precisely how schooling itself infringes upon both thought and action. But parents, teachers, and students are still stuck in schools 100 years out of date. They are trying to make changes that should have been made decades ago and are now too tardy to be of use. Yet they still must fight to make them, for what else can they do? That was the situation in New Orleans. The local audience had come to learn how to make small, difficult, and necessary changes, while many of the speakers had already discarded those changes as being essentially useless, reactionary, and wasteful. The experts were hoping to move their listeners to a general reconsideration of the whole problem. But the necessary connections between people were made imperfectly, fitfully, and what became increasingly clear was the growing distance between thought about education and the reality of the schools, and how we flounder in the space between them.

Now, rereading that piece, I find that I would put things a bit differently. The differences I mention are no doubt there, and they are not trivial ones, but in some way, at a distance, they seem complementary and not antagonistic. Things are so awful now for the young that it does not matter much where one chooses to help them—in or out of schools—so long as that help involves an increase for them in independence and choice. I used to think that was possible only outside the state's schools, but that view now seems too absolute, too luxurious. Certainly teachers like Jim Herndon or Herb Kohl seem able to bring into the schools, like a smuggled drug, enough reality to remind the students about what is waiting out there, beyond the institution's limits, for those stubborn enough to seek it out. And though I do not think that the schools can be changed by that activity in any permanent way, it is no doubt better for the young than nothing at all, for they need good company so badly that it does not matter where or how they get it.

In the same way, even more importantly, the schools of thought I have described as existential and political do not seem to me opposed to one another. Both of them are attempts to restore to the young what has been taken from them. The simple fact is that the school works in two realms simultaneously, destroying at the same time the inner integrity of the psyche and the outer community of relation. Both areas are corroded, occupied, diminished. What happens is simply that the hold of institutions is established by the systematic destruction of *all* relation, public or private, that might give the individual a place to stand over and against the institution. The process is neither exclusively political nor existential. It is both; both the inner and outer worlds are affected.

The result is a kind of doubled blindness, a doubled encapsulation, the loss of two kinds of potency: animal potency and political potency. The corrosion of each realm affects the other. The institutionalization of imagination and feeling creates a void in which the institution becomes all-powerful, thereby occupying the space that would ordinarily be filled by voluntary cooperation and association. And the institutionalization of association and community deprives the individual of felt connection, real human sustenance—a loss which is experienced inside as private, existential pain. The two realms and the two kinds of loss are so interdependent and intertwined that it is impossible to see either of them singly or to grant either one more importance than the other.

At bottom, then, the two views I have described are both necessary, for each of them is an incomplete response to an institutional process which is felt by the individual, the student, as a single condition, no matter how we break it down in the ways we analyze or respond to it. In the privacy of the psyche and the individual life our distinctions break down, melt back into a general experience, an undifferentiated feeling; the individual simply feels adrift and cut off, and it is that single condition, the pervasive weather of being, which makes most students so susceptible to the control of institutions. Where else, after all, can they find a place to belong?

I remember, years ago, when I taught in college, how I was surprised at first by the states of mind of the students, most of whom seemed to have been so deprived of things, and so confused by that deprivation, that they could no longer think or feel clearly. I remember making notes for myself, trying to describe that condition, coming back again and again, unconsciously, to the metaphors I have used here:

> For my students, significance and meaning are always somewhere in the distance, somewhere in the future, located across immense valleys and mountains, and they could only reach them by slogging across *time*, trudging for years from class to class in the hope of earning admittance to what they have been taught is culture or society. There is far more to it than simply acquiring the skills and credentials necessary for a job. It has something to do with existence itself, as if my students have been systematically bled of their own existence by institutions, and now must earn it back through obedience and service. They have in that sense been denied personhood, have been denied substance and depth for there is no substance to the person, no depth, except for what accumulates as experience—*and is somehow received by the world itself*, and it is precisely that reception which is missing in the schools. Some of us are lucky enough to find comrades and lovers who legitimize and ground what we are, but somehow our solidity as persons is always a battle between the receptivity of our friends and the denials of the institution: we are fed by one process and bled by the other. So my students are uncertain of themselves, contemporary versions of Eliot's hollow men and women, as if they have been turned inside and shaken out. Knowledge, meaning, information, discipline . . . it all

comes from the outside, pouring in. The person has been sucked out and then buffeted by wave upon wave of demand and rhetoric—the great internal spaces of solitude and silence somehow broken and invaded and shrunk. What is left of the person seems invariably stiffened into a defensive posture and huddled protectively in some small cave of the soul, unwilling to come out.

They have been swindled into believing that the schools and society and knowledge are somehow identical—and they do not seem sufficiently convinced of their own intuitions, passions and strengths to make judgments about them or create alternatives to them. Many of them feel exactly about school the way young men do about the army. They are not in schools because they think they can find anything of use; they are there simply because they don't know what else to do. Life without institutional sanction and meaning has ceased to be life for them, for it is no longer possible for them to locate themselves in meaningful ways without having their existence legitimized by the structure of institutions. Simply put: they have been mesmerized at the deepest levels of imagination, then partially awakened—with only a dim memory of what it might feel like to define things for oneself, to feel meaning as a light and depth within the self.

And what is the alternative to that?

As I look through my notes I find this sentence: "I look up after class and see on the blackboard only one word, the word *dance*"; ideally, all learning is a kind of dance—one in which we perceive the world anew in the gestures we make. I remember the first stanza in Yeats' poem, "Among School Children."

> The children learn to cipher and to sing.
> To study reading-books and histories,
> To cut and sew, be neat in everything
> In the best modern way—

And then, the last:

> Labour is blossoming or dancing where
> The body is not bruised to pleasure soul,
> Nor beauty born out of its own despair,
> Nor blear-eyed wisdom out of midnight oil.
> O chestnut-tree, great-rooted blossomer,
> Are you the leaf, the blossom or the bole?
> O body swayed to music, O brightening glance,
> How can we know the dancer from the dance?

To cut and sew; The dancer and the dance. Those are the opposing ways open to us, and there is an immense distance between them. The institutional way is always cutting and sewing, patching together the segmented parts of a reality already destroyed by the institution itself. And in the other way, the way we have lost, the body *is* a dancer, moving to its own time and rhythm and steadily deepening, ripening; it *is* a process, and we are inseparable from the process of change, the steady evolution of identity. We are simply its furthest edge, a twist in life which perceives itself as "I" and moves forward naturally with the creaturely grace of change. Wisdom is really a gesture, the natural sap of being alive, the intelligent shape given to aliveness, and it is not separable from things, does not come from outside of us, cannot be taught or learned, but is simply *in* life, infusing when it is found whatever we say or do.

It is no accident that Yeats chooses a natural metaphor, that of the tree, to express it, because that world *is* the world of nature, the natural world, and it exists not only around but also inside of us as the inner direction of all organic life, a kind of natural ripening which moves us always toward immersion and participation in the world—which is where and how knowledge begins. Our schools have never been the source of such knowledge, nor have they been the source of relation or ripening; those are rooted elsewhere; they seem almost coded in the flesh beyond all volition. What I meant to suggest in my notes was the nature of precisely the thing that the schools destroy: the felt connections which lie at the heart of all wisdom and which are by no means at odds with other kinds of knowing, but without which they become destructive, mere modes of separation and loss. What I mean is difficult to describe, and is perhaps nothing less than a felt love of the world, the kind of quiet grace that shows up in literature in the essays Camus wrote about the people of Oran, or in books like Giono's *The Joy of Man's Desiring* or Paustovsky's *Story of a Life*. Perhaps the most obvious examples I can think of appear in Tolstoy's work, and perhaps it is no accident that his ideas about education play a part in the history of free schools. The best examples I know occur in *War and Peace*: first, Prince Bolkonsky's discovery on the battlefield, as he stares into the sky, that he is still alive, and then his reaction to the great oak blooming once again in the wood, late in the spring, after winter and apparent death. In each case, wisdom is not simply the function of revelation or experience, but of connection, almost an identification with the rhythms and cycles of nature, something at work both outside and inside the self, a habitation running deeper than individual thought or social role. So too, in *Anna Karenina,* Levin comes closest to the heart of life when he joins the peasants cutting grain. Lost in heat and light and the muscular rhythms of his own body at work, hip-deep in the grain and in the company of comrades, he transcends all consciousness of self and draws from the world, as if through his pores, a wisdom waiting for him there, something already inside him but until then unrealized.

That is what I am talking about here: the lessons of relation. But I am not talking merely about relation to oneself or to a few others, what we call "personal" or "human" relations. That is only a part of human need. I mean, instead, the whole range of human relation and need: the natural creaturely appetite for civic, cultural and communal relation, for free association, for cooperation and community—the activities Kropotkin joined together under the heading of "mutual aid." Those too are needs so deeply rooted that they seem as instinctive and as biologically determined as any other appetite. Writing about the Athenian polis and the state, Hannah Arendt had this to say about the Greeks:

> ... the principal characteristic of the tyrant was that he deprived the citizen of access to the public realm, where he could show himself, see and be seen, hear and be heard, that he prohibited the *agoreuein* and *politeuein,* confined the citizens to the privacy of their households. . . . According to the Greeks, to be banished to the privacy of household life was tantamount to being deprived of the specifically human potentialities of life. . . .

The same thing is true of all of us, although we do not all know it. The denial of the social impulse—that is, the loss of self-determination, of a company of equals, of an open world, of unmanaged experience—is not only a *political* experience; it is also a loss of nature, a denial of human nature, and it is felt, internally, as a loss of being, a loss of self.

What I mean to say, then, is that the restoration of relation means its restoration in all realms, in both the private and public worlds, and for that reason, as I have said, the essays collected here form a coherent whole. Each of them is an attempt to restore to human habitation a realm now occupied by the state; each of them is an attempt to enlarge both the persons and the world. For Kozol that means a change in consciousness, political power and social justice; for Goodman it means independent choice, the end to state domination, authenticity of behavior; for Sylvia Ashton-Warner it means the reactivation of imagination; for Herndon it means the ability to enter and accept the realities of day-to-day experience; for Illich it means an end to institutionalization and a return to what he elsewhere calls "conviviality," almost a Christian love. But whatever the alternatives or tactics suggested, the underlying aim remains the same: to release the possibilities of individual growth and human community, to re-occupy the realms now in the state's possession or excluded by the state's version of reality. And by "state" at this point I mean more than a system of government or a bureaucratic organization; I mean the entire cast of thought which is encouraged by institutions and which we have internalized and projected upon all of reality: the ways in which the world, in our minds, has ceased to be an open, living realm.

The Greeks that Hannah Arendt described also had a state, but theirs (in both senses still), at least for a short while, was unlike ours. For a few generations (leaving aside the question of who belonged to the polity), all those who belonged to the polity felt themselves to be free, equal and responsible. No one was over them, and their world, far more than ours, was a "horizontal" one, opening out. They had no bureaucracy, no fixed corps of higher officials, no hierarchy. The state was identical with those who composed it, was a community of persons, not an abstract entity or overarching myth. They chose their officials by lot, regardless of age or experience, assuming that all were capable of governing and had the right to do it. Decisions were collective, made in meetings open to all. Public life was understood as the natural right, and what learning meant to them was "participation" in it; the entire polis and city were understood to be educational; one learned by doing, by being in the world.

It did not last long, of course; nor did it apply to all persons; women, slaves and tradesmen were excluded. But I use it here only as an example of a moment in history in which, for a while, the screen and dream of empire did not come between persons and their comrades or the world. One can think of many other examples, ranging from the Bushmen and Pygmy tribes and their immersion in the world of nature (for the Pygmy the forest itself is a god; the Bushmen listen to the stars) to those rare moments in more "civilized" nations in which the world opens up and out: a short period in the French Revolution, the first few years of the American republic, the period in Barcelona described by Orwell in Homage to Catalonia, a few months in Mexico when in 1911 the Zapatistas had taken Morelos and were running it communally. I mention those almost at random, and there are many others of course, and most of those are not "historical" or earthshaking; many of them are domestic, private, as simple as lovemaking or meditation, all of them moments in which life moves us past all control (all hierarchial control) and into another relation to things, which means, in a sense, another world.

And it is that, finally, that these essays are about. They are about such moments and the possibility of such moments. They will not tell us how to change the schools, because the schools are beyond real change. They will not tell us how to do away with schools or what to do instead of using them, for not enough people can yet imagine life without them to move past them in any widespread way. And yet it is because of that fact, not in spite of it, that these essays are important. They remind us about what is possible; in the midst of occupied territory they clear at least a small space, sometimes through action, sometimes in the mind. I will try to put it as succinctly as I can. At this point in time the power of institutions can only be diminished by imaginative thought or action, but the sources of such thought or action cannot be found in pedagogy or pedagogical reform. One must find them instead in experience itself, outside pedagogy, in what I have called "the world." But that means that one must be devoted enough to the world, must like it enough, to move towards it, to let it in. The essays here are examples of that kind of devotion. They are examples of thought and action rooted not in pedagogy, but in a devotion to the world. They encourage us to move past habit and rhetoric into the world, and that too is what I meant at the beginning of this piece by "freedom."

—Peter Marin

FREE SCHOOLS
AND THEIR ROOTS

The essays which open this collection are by George Dennison and Jonathan Kozol. Together, they offer an explanation not only of free schools, but of the main ideas at work in the radical education movement. Both Kozol and Dennison are working teachers, and they have concentrated their attention on ghetto children. Dennison's background has been largely therapeutic; he, like Neill and also Paul Goodman, has been influenced by Freud, Reich and other analytical approaches. Kozol's concerns are more political. His approach is based in large part on the work of Paulo Freire, a radical South American educator who stresses the relationship of literacy and liberation, and in whose eyes education and language itself can be instruments of either oppression or revolution, depending entirely upon the ways in which they are taught. In that sense, both writers are in agreement; it is simply that Dennison seems to see oppression and liberation in emotional and energetic terms, and Kozol sees them in social and political terms.

As for free schools in general, they are attempts to replace education-as-oppression with a liberating education. In the past several years, hundreds of free schools have been begun across the country. At the moment there are perhaps four hundred in existence, ranging from the kinds of ghetto school described by Dennison to almost hermetic mountain communes. Because so many of the schools are short-lived, the number of schools now operating indicates many more beginnings and disappearances, and it is impossible to estimate how many schools or even *kinds* of schools have been established before closing down. The main problems which have plagued them are lack of money and students, and that is due, of course, to the state's monopolization of educational funds.

But beyond that lies the whole range of problems which arise because free schools, as a form, are untried and unexplored, and the people in them must make them up as they go along, learning from scratch what will and will not work in a variety of situations and communities.

In that sense, all free schools are "experimental." They comprise a collectively autotelic experience in which the participants are learning, for the first time, how to exist on their own, outside of institutional limits, without their support and structure. For that reason alone the schools are usually turbulent and exhausting places, often no better than the public schools. They fail to "work" right; they don't satisfy the expectations of either teachers or students; adults often impose upon the young absurd ideas and ideologies; children, given more freedom, act in unexpected and disturbing ways, learn only with difficulty how to learn independently. The entire school, the *act* of being in it, running it, becomes the educational experience; the school can no longer disguise itself as the "container" of learning; the difficulties in keeping it going, running it, making it work, become the subject matter, the curriculum. But all of that, after all, is to be expected. Most people in free schools are trying to live for the first time in their lives in a communal way on their own terms. Stepping past the limits of institutions, they tend to discover suddenly that they have brought those limits with them, have long ago internalized the institutions they had hoped to escape. They exist in them still in expectation and habit, and much of the turbulence in the free schools is the result of the need to get rid of those inner limits, to move past them a second time.

And yet, despite those difficulties and also because of them, free schools are important. It is there, for instance, that people discover that what they had taken for granted within the institution as personality and "normal" behavior was simply a depressed habituation to a closed situation. Once beyond it, many students and adults begin to perceive things in different terms altogether, to understand a bit more about the possibilities of community and freedom, to feel them, inside, as a sense of exhilaration and power—a *physical* change in the way things are experienced. The world is literally transformed, becoming simultaneously more open, more extensive, more promising and more dangerous. If it is not necessarily "better" or more comfortable, it is at least alive, and interesting, and that in itself is worth the trouble. What's more, the ideas and changes in perception generated by the free schools enter the larger culture and even the public schools by a kind of osmosis, and they act there as a goad to action and change. Many of the reforms made in the public schools have been the diminished imitations of a freedom established more genuinely in the free schools. And, finally, the free schools— along with other independent oases like communes, community-action groups, etc.—keep alive in the culture the idea of people doing things for themselves and together. They substitute for the idea of hierarchy and exclusive expertise a sense of communal competence and cooperative invention, and they remind us all, if only in a small way, that we can act more independently than we do.

One final note about the free schools. They will continue to have trouble surviving as long as the state continues to monopolize the money spent on education. It is largely through that monopolization that the state controls where the young go to school and what they learn, and also, of course, where teachers can work and what they must teach. Most parents, having paid once, through taxes, for their children's education, are reluctant to put out any more money for schooling, even when they can afford it, and most of the time they can't. In that simple way, the state forces the young to attend the public schools and forces the teachers to teach there. Now, in a few communities, experiments are being conducted with what is called the "voucher system." Parents are given vouchers by the state worth a certain amount of money toward their children's education. They may spend that voucher on any school they choose, and the schools then turn in the vouchers to the state and are reimbursed. Thus, the state, having taken the money from the parents, puts it back in their hands to spend as they wish, and that new money, now in circulation, gives the free schools a chance to compete with public schools.

There are other changes too that might be made. In Denmark, for instance, any group of fifty parents desiring to start a school for their children can petition the state for funding. That seems simple and sensible, and if we tried the same thing in this country we would (1) begin to break the hold of the myth of public schooling on the mind and (2) be able to assess more clearly just how much appeal the free schools have, and just how deeply people feel dissatisfied with the public schools. But the fact of the matter is that we do not yet collectively want to break the hold of public schooling or make it possible for parents to choose against them easily, and until we do, the free schools will stay in the same condition they are in now. They will struggle for existence, pop up and die out, will remain, in essence, an "amateur" activity in the worst and best senses of that word: uneven, chaotic and yet, always, acts of some kind of will, some kind of love, rather than the result of habit and coercion.

GEORGE DENNISON
From: The Lives of Children

There is no need to add to the criticism of our public schools. The critique is extensive and can hardly be improved on. . . .

The question now is what to do. In the pages that follow, I would like to describe one unfamiliar approach to the problems which by now have become familiar. And since "the crisis of the schools" consists in reality of a great many crises in the lives of children, I shall try to make the children of the First Street School the real subject of this book. There were twenty-three black, white, and Puerto Rican in almost equal proportions, all from low-income families in New York's Lower East Side. About half were on welfare. About half, too, had come to us from the public schools with severe learning and behavior problems.

Four things about the First Street School were unusual: first, its small size and low teacher/pupil ratio; second, the fact that this luxurious intimacy, which is ordinarily very expensive, cost about the same per child as the $850 annual operating costs of the public schools; third, our reversal of conventional structure, for where the public school conceives of itself merely as a place of instruction, and puts severe restraints on the relationships between persons, we conceived of ourselves as an environment for growth, and accepted the relationships between the children and ourselves as being the very heart of the school; and fourth, the kind of freedom experienced by teachers and pupils alike.

Freedom is an abstract and terribly elusive word. I hope that a context of examples will make its meaning clear. The question is not really one of authority, though it is usually argued in that form. When adults give up authority, the freedom of children is not necessarily increased. Freedom is not motion in a vacuum, but motion in a continuum. If we want

From *The Lives of Children,* by George Dennison. Copyright © 1969 by George Dennison. Reprinted by permission of Random House, Inc.

to know what freedom is, we must discover what the continuum is. "The principle," Dewey remarks, "is not what justifies an activity, for the principle is but another name for the continuity of the activity." We might say something similar of freedom: The mother of a child in a public school told me that he kept complaining. "They never let me *finish* anything!" We might say of the child that he lacked important freedoms, but his own expression is closer to the experience: activities important to him remained unfulfilled. Our concern for freedom is our concern for fulfillment—of activities we deem important and of persons we know are unique. To give freedom means to stand out of the way of the formative powers possessed by others.

Before telling more of the school, I must say that I was a partisan of libertarian values even before working there. I had read of the schools of A. S. Neill and Leo Tolstoy. I had worked in the past with severely disturbed children, and had come to respect the integrity of the organic processes of growth, which given the proper environment are the one source of change in individual lives. And so I was biased from the start and cannot claim the indifference of a neutral observer. Events at school did, however, time and again, confirm the beliefs I already held—which, I suppose, leaves me still a partisan, though convinced twice over. Yet if I can prove nothing at all in a scientific sense, there is still a power of persuasion in the events themselves, and I can certainly hope that our experience will arouse an experimental interest in other parents and teachers.

But there is something else that I would like to convey, too, and this is simply a sense of the lives of those who were involved—the jumble of persons and real events which did in fact constitute our school. The closer one comes to the facts of life, the less exemplary they seem, but the more human and the richer. Something of our time in history and our place in the world belong to Vicente screaming in the hallway, and José opening the blade of a ten-inch knife—even more than to Vicente's subsequent learning to cooperate and José to read. So, too, with other apparently small details: the fantasy life and savagery of the older boys, the serenity and rationality of the younger ones, teachers' moments of doubt and defeat. Learning, in its essentials, is not a distinct and separate process. It is a function of growth. We took it quite seriously in this light, and found ourselves getting more and more involved in individual lives. It seems likely to me that the actual features of this involvement may prove useful to other people. At the same time, I would like to try to account for the fact that almost all of our children improved markedly, and some few spectacularly. We were obviously doing something right, and I would like to hazard a few guesses at what it might have been. All instruction was individual, and that was obviously a factor. The improvement I am speaking of, however, was not simply a matter of learning, but of radical changes in character. Where Vicente had been withdrawn and destructive, he became an eager participant in group activities and ceased destroying everything he touched. Both Eléna and Maxine had been thieves and were incredibly rebellious. After several months they could be trusted and had become imaginative and responsible contributors at school meetings. Such changes as these are not accomplished by instruction. They proceed from broad environmental causes. Here again, details which may seem irrelevant to the business of a school will give the reader an idea of what these causes may have been. A better way of saying this is that the business of a school is not, or should not be, mere instruction, but the life of the child.

This is especially important under such conditions as we experience today. Life in our country is chaotic and corrosive, and the time of childhood for many millions is difficult and harsh. It will not be an easy matter to bring our berserk technocracy under control, but we *can* control the environment of the schools. It is a relatively small environment and has always been structured by deliberation. If, as parents, we were to take as our concern not the instruction of our children, but the lives of our children, we would find that our schools could be used in a powerfully regenerative way. Against all that is shoddy and violent and treacherous and emotionally impoverished in American life, we might propose conventions which were rational and straightforward, rich both in feeling and thought, and which treated individuals with a respect we do little more at present than proclaim from our public rostrums. We might cease thinking of school as a place, and learn to believe that it is basically relationships: between children and adults, adults and adults, children and other children. The four walls and the principal's office would cease to loom so hugely as the essential ingredients.

It is worth mentioning here that, with two exceptions, the parents of the children at First Street were not libertarians. They thought that they believed in compulsion, and rewards and punishments, and formal discipline, and report cards, and homework, and elaborate school facilities. They looked rather askance at our noisy classrooms and informal relations. If they persisted in sending us their children, it was not because they agreed with our methods, but because they were desperate. As the months went by, however, and the children who had been truants now attended eagerly, and those who had been failing now began to learn, the parents drew their own conclusions. By the end of the first year there was a high morale among them, and great devotion to the school.

We had no administrators. We were small and didn't need them. The parents found that, after all, they approved of this. They themselves could judge the competence of the teachers, and so could their children—by the specific act of learning. The parents' past experience of administrators had been uniformly upsetting—and the proof, of course, was in the pudding: the children were happier and *were* learning. As for the children, they never missed them.

We did not give report cards. We knew each child, knew his capacities and his problems, and the vagaries of his growth. This knowledge could not be recorded on little cards. The parents found—again—that they approved of this. It diminished the blind anxieties of life, for grades had never meant much to them anyway except some dim sense of *problem*, or some dim reassurance that things were all right. When they wanted to know how their children were doing, they simply asked the teachers.

We didn't give tests, at least not of the competitive kind. It was important to be aware of what the children knew, but more important to be aware of *how* each child knew what he knew. We could learn nothing about Maxine by testing Eléna. And so there was no comparative testing at all. The children never missed those invidious comparisons, and the teachers were spared the absurdity of ranking dozens of personalities on one uniform scale.

Our housing was modest. The children came to school in play-torn clothes. Their families were poor. A torn dress, torn pants, frequent cleanings—there were expenses they could not afford. Yet how can children play without getting dirty? Our uncleanliness standard was just right. It looked awful and suited everyone.

We treated the children with consideration and justice. I don't mean that we never got angry and never yelled at them (nor they at us). I mean that we took seriously the pride of life that belongs to the young—even to the very young. We did not coerce them in violation of their proper independence. Parents and children both found that they approved very much of this.

Now I would like to describe the school, or more correctly, the children and teachers. I shall try to bring out in detail three important things:

>1) That the proper concern of a primary school is not education in a narrow sense, and still less preparation for later life, but the present lives of the children—a point made repeatedly by John Dewey, and very poorly understood by many of his followers.
>
>2) That when the conventional routines of a school are abolished (the military discipline, the schedules, the punishments and rewards, the standardization), what arises is neither a vacuum nor chaos, but rather a new order, based first on relationships between adults and children, and children and their peers, but based ultimately on such truths of the human condition as these: that the mind does not function separately from the emotions, but thought partakes of feeling and feeling of thought; that there is no such thing as knowledge *per se*, knowledge in a vacuum, but rather all knowledge is possessed and must be expressed by individuals; that the human voices preserved in books belong to the real features of the world, and that children are so powerfully attracted to this world that the very motion of their curiosity comes through to us as a form of love; that an active moral life cannot be evolved except where people are free to express their feelings and act upon the insights of conscience.
>
>3) That running a primary school—*provided it be small*—is an extremely

From: The Lives of Children 23

simple thing. It goes without saying that the teachers must be competent (which does not necessarily mean passing courses in a teacher's college). Given this *sine qua non*, there is nothing mysterious. The present quagmire of public education is entirely the result of unworkable centralization and the lust for control that permeates every bureaucratic institution.

In saying this, I do not mean that the work in a free school is easy. On the contrary, teachers find it taxing. But they find it rewarding, too— quite unlike the endless round of frustrations experienced by those at work in the present system.

    *   *   *

In our own time, the most important example of freedom in education has been A. S. Neill's Summerhill School in England. It is a residence school—a community, really—and its laws and customs are worked out by all participants. In spite of the great popularity of Neill's book, *Summerhill: A Radical Approach to Child Rearing,* the school itself still has an undeserved reputation for anarchy. Its distinctiveness lies actually not in the absence of regulations, but in the kinds of regulations it makes use of and in its manner of arriving at them. There is a General School Meeting every Saturday night. All questions pertaining to the life of the community are discussed here and are settled by vote. Where certain kinds of rules (e.g., bedtime regulations for the young) tend to survive in one basic form, others are changed frequently or refined. Penalties are extremely specific. One lonely boy, for example, was cured of stealing when his fellows voted to give him money for each offense.

But there is no need to describe Summerhill here. Interested persons will have read the book, which in its paperback edition was a long-term best seller in this country. I would like to quote from John Holt's description of the school, however, as it appeared in the *Bulletin* of the Summerhill Society, U.S.A., in 1965:

> It was the young children, six, seven, and eight, who made the strongest impression on me. The older children, though free, seemed not to have had their freedom long enough to be able to relax with it and take it for granted. The little ones were quite different. Occasionally, very rarely, in a particularly happy family, I have seen little children who have seemed wholly secure, at ease, natural, and happy. But never before this meeting had I seen so many of them in one place, least of all in a school. They were joyous, spontaneous, unaffected. I wondered why this should be, and at the party I thought I saw why. More times than I could count, I would see a little child come up to a big one, and with a word, or a gesture, or a clutch of the hand, claim his attention. I never saw one rebuffed, or treated anything but lovingly. The big kids were always picking them up, hugging them, swinging them around, dancing with them, carrying them on their shoulders. For the little children, Summerhill was a world full of big people, all of whom could be enjoyed, trusted, and counted on. It was like living in an enormous family, but without the rivalries and

jealousies that too often plague our too small and too possessive families. . . .

One of the rules is that bedtime in the cottage, where the little kids live, is at 8:30. Further down the page I read another rule, obviously passed under pressure of necessity: "All kissing good-night involving cottagers must be over by 8:30."

The two issues most frequently discussed by persons who are interested in Summerhill—either for or against—are its sexual mores and the children's freedom to stay away from classes.

In sexual matters, Neill's point of view is a simple one: the evils of repression can be avoided. We are not *sexual* beings, but human beings. Sexuality cannot be excluded from our lives; neither will it dominate our lives under conditions of freedom. Neill detests pornography, prurience, and priggishness. To be antisex is to be antilife.

In short, sex is not treated as an evil at Summerhill. In fact—so I infer from Neill's pages, and so I gather from talks with Summerhill alumnae —it is not much "treated" at all. The boys and girls are let alone. One might say that Nature takes its course, but the fact is that Nature always takes its course. I doubt if there is any more sex at Summerhill than at American high schools, but certainly the air is cleaner than ours, the lives of the students freer of cant and hypocrisy and lame-duck psychology.

Neill speaks often of the "free child," and in many respects his book is intended as a manual of child-rearing. The idea of sexual freedom is not a Neillian idea. We hear it instead from the mouths of his critics and of some few disciples he himself has declared he wished he did not possess. One of Neill's great virtues is that he keeps his eyes on persons. We tend to do the opposite here in America, and lose ourselves among issues. The distinction is crucial in practice, and is worth going into in some detail.

The phrase "sexual freedom," like almost every phrase involving the word freedom, is a polemical abstraction. Its background is a long series of heated arguments. When we turn from these arguments to the phenomena of lives, we see immediately that what we call "freedom" is not ours to give, and what we call "sexuality" cannot be defined by kissing, caressing, and making love. I have listened to arguments about sexual freedom at conferences sponsored by the Summerhill Society in New York. They were often touching, almost always excited and urgent. Adults cannot speak of this issue except in tones of longing, regret, resentment, anxiety, bitterness. One finds housewives in the audience who seem to be speaking of their children, but whose tones and facial expressions are saying, "I am yearning for love! Absolve me of my sexual guilt!"; and others who, in effect, cry bitterly, "I was denied it, and by God I won't grant it to anyone else!" Some speak with sadness and regret, and soon find themselves reassuring the anxious ones. Both band together and attack the authoritarians in their midst. I have observed all this when adolescent students were also present. One had only to look at their faces to understand the truth: they preferred the dignity of being let alone, but come what may, they would certainly fuck. Nor were they interested in sexual freedom, but in Jane and Harriet, LeRoy and Dick. Love, after all, is love. It may tolerate poets, but *spokesmen* are anathema, whether they're *for* or *against*.

Yet these young persons were extremely interested in the arguments. There was something they shared immediately with the adults.

Aside from regret for the past, and the anxious fear of regret itself, the adults were not speaking (either pro or con) of the actual behavior of particular young persons. They were speaking of their own willingness to sanction sexuality, or their desire to confine it. Nor were the young who were present worried very much that their own pleasures would be denied them. They would outwit the adults, as always. They would climb out windows and down rainspouts; they would tell lies, etc. Yet they, too, were extremely interested, and their interest was similarly in the question of sanction.

Sanction is not a matter of *what happens*, but of methods of control and ideals of life: what sort of world must we build? The young understand this question with great immediacy. And they want a great deal more than sexual freedom. They want *wholeness*. They do not want to lie and evade and suffer guilt, but to affirm themselves in the largest possible harmony of self and society, passion and intellect, duty and pleasure. They want the esteem of their elders, and they cannot help but want the excitement that rises so imperiously in their own experience. They know very well, too, that where sanction is involved, the attitudes of a few teachers are mere grains on a sandy shore. The problem begins in infancy and runs through the whole of society. Mere slogans and attitudes are of little value, and there is a terrible, naive hubris in the behavior of a teacher who believes that he can sanction sexuality by conferring freedom. He can no more sanction it than sanction the law of gravity. All he can do is cease to attempt to control the young. Beyond this he can ally himself with the student's quest for wholeness. Here the teacher's own quest for wholeness is extremely valuable. Life being what it is, there is no man who can stand before the young and acclaim himself an exemplar of liberated energies. The "do as I do" cannot be put in this form, for if he boasts of sexual freedom, the young will wonder about the propaganda: why does he boast? Why is so much energy devoted precisely to polemics? A good example of this attitude can be found in the writings of Henry Miller, which carry a heavy theme of sexual and self-liberation. One observes, however, that the liberated self constructs a peculiar and hermetic environment, one of proselytizing: endless rhapsodies on liberation, preaching freedom in order to retain the illusion of it. The loss is obvious: it is the world. Euphoria, in this context, might be defined as anxiety masquerading as pride.

In life, as in art, the healing truth is the whole truth. The libertarian teacher cannot give freedom. He can only cease to control. He cannot sanction sexuality. He can only seek to allay guilt. He cannot eradicate sexual embarrassment either in himself or in his students by an act of will, but he *can* identify embarrassment as a problem, just as he can hold forth a human ideal in which hatred of the body, distrust of emotion, and repugnance toward sex will find no part. At best, the libertarian can demonstrate reason, faith, generosity, and hope struggling against the damages he himself has already sustained and which he hopes to mitigate in the lives of his students. This is a far cry from the banner-waving of sexual freedom. Let me give an example to make this more plain.

I visited a school ostensibly modeled on Summerhill, but in fact (so I believe) not much like it. I noticed two teen-agers who were pathologically depressed. I learned that they were suffering severe conflicts with their parents. I was informed, too, that their parents were small-minded, narrow, repressive, status-seeking petit bourgeois; which is to say that the suffering of the two students had been invested with a programmatic, radical meaning; their destestation of their parents appeared as a form of loyalty to the school. The two students, in short, were in a hopeless quandary, being tugged in opposite directions by self-interested adults. To make matters worse, the tugging at school was largely *sub rosa*, implicit rather than overt, and the foreground was filled by "freedom," that is, by lack of contact, lack of guidance, lack of structure, lack of everything that children experiencing such disorders absolutely require. Let me hasten to say that such lacks as these cannot be filled by rules and regulations. They must be filled by persons, and not just any persons, but those capable of true encounter and decently motivated for work with the young. The problem at this school was that the director himself regarded staff and students less as people than as events in his own protracted crusade against middle-class America. The faculty, too, consisted of True Believers, and I had never before seen such a listless, resentful bunch, or heard the words "creativity" and "spontaneity" bandied about quite so often.

When the young are experiencing conflicts within themselves, it is disastrous for the teacher to "take sides"; and no vice is more prevalent among teachers than taking sides against the parents. What the student needs is not an ally in one quarter of his own psychic economy—which tends to perpetuate his conflict precisely as conflict—but an ally in the world. This is what I mean by supporting his quest for wholeness. It is the difference between saying, "You are right to detest your parents," and saying, "You are obviously suffering because you detest your parents." It is the difference between saying, "Transcend your sexual guilt! Be free!" and saying, "Let us take your guilt seriously. How do you experience it?" I am not suggesting that every teacher be a psychotherapist. I am insisting that every teacher put himself in relation with the person before him, and not with one portion of that person's conflicts. Just to the extent that a teacher will do this, he will recognize, too, that sexuality permeates everything. It cannot be set aside and given special treatment. When, in the classroom, the child is allowed to speak freely and experience the creative unity of feelings, hunches, thoughts, humor, etc., we are in fact supporting a positive sexuality. When we create conditions which do away with shame and self-contempt, we are supporting a positive sexuality. And so on.

The notion of sexual freedom, in short, is another of many symptoms of the massive sickness of our world. It is not an idea we can use, but an idea that needs to be dissolved until its atoms come to rest again in the phenomena of life. It would be helpful, too, to recognize that sexuality is a world phenomenon, not merely an individual one. There is an ecology of the emotions. No better example can be found than that of the hippies of New York's East Village. They are remarkably good-looking and sweet-natured young people. They believe earnestly in sexual freedom and the beauty of the human body. And they act upon their beliefs. But alas! alas! the erotic élan of youth simply isn't there. And all their modest or desperate bravery, and their earnest believing, cannot put it there. The conditions of their lives are decisive. Their lot is anxious, insecure, badly nourished, cut off from the future, alienated from the past, anonymous in the present. They are haunted by the bomb and deadened by crises of identity. Where will the joy of life come from? Another example, showing again the meager role of opinion where such broad, primitive phenomena as sexuality are involved: I attended a showing at an avant-garde film house, and after the main course a little divertissement was thrown on the screen for laughs, one of those all-girl-orchestra shorts of the early 1930's, two dozen marimba players in low-cut gowns and long-enduring smiles. Members of the audience (not all, for I think some must have felt as I did) laughed complacently at their provincial style and the bouncy banality of their music. None of that meant much to me. I was absolutely astonished at the sensual appearance of those girls. Their smiles were in fact naive smiles of pleasure, their eyes were bright, their faces vivacious, their arms and shoulders softly rounded and relaxed, and there was something melting and fluid in the way their torsos rode upon their hips. Would any one of them have come out for sexual freedom? One might well suppose that they had few attitudes at all, and if asked would simply affirm for the moment the most conventional—and by our standards, retrograde—morality. But that was prewar America, not yet so hugely organized, rich in space and time, the future undarkened by the bomb or the present by unending war, hot and cold. I need not list the differences. Flesh and psyche were simply better off, and they certainly looked it. The lights went on and the girls in the audience stood up, adjusting their plastic coats and mini-skirts. Some were still smiling. All most likely were digesting the Pill they had taken that morning. And how put-upon they looked! I do not mean that they were spiritless. Not at all. There was something strong in them, something admirable. But the verve and color was all in their clothes. Their eyes were lightless or fixed, their faces drawn tight by lines of strain. Tension showed in their throats and the unyielding motions of their gaits. Some, no doubt, had a style in bed, as they had a style in clothes and a style in cars. They would quite routinely speak in affirmation of sex, and confess to the psychotherapist that the issue was not sex but meaning, joy, life, passion, love, and describe a nightmare of growing cold, not unrelated to the style of being "cool." As for the therapist, he will have heard the identical story, in essence, a thousand times. These tales are not produced by family strife alone, or by America destroying itself in isolation. They are the landscape of the modern world.

If we want to release and sustain and civilize, in the true sense, the sexuality of the young, we can begin by putting sexuality back into the person. It is the whole child we are interested in. We can increase his security, treat him with justice and consideration, respect his pride of life, value the independence of his spirit, be his ally in a world that needs to be changed. We can do nothing—more directly than this—about his sexuality.

The practice at Summerhill is a case in point. The security of the individual, his constructive role in the community, the absence of punishment and coercion, the student's responsible awareness of other lives—these things taken together promote a healthy, positive sexuality for the same reason that they promote unusual courtesy (many visitors have remarked on this) and vigorous self-reliance: the whole person is encouraged to flourish. If many problems still remain, it is not surprising, since Summerhill is a small part of a large and troubled world.

Nor is it odd that some few of Neill's disciples should have distorted his meaning. This happens inevitably to every innovator, which is another way of saying that Neill is not a Summerhillian, any more than Freud was a Freudian, or Reich a Reichian. Pioneers of this kind emerge into history in severe conflict with the value systems of their youth. In their own persons they represent profound resolutions of conflicting experience. Their conflicts, however, tend to become background. I mean that their chief appearance in the writing is a stylistic one. Freud, for example, was adopted as the patron saint of the French surrealists, but after an interview with Breton, refused to take seriously their use of his insights. They had not understood him. For one thing they had paid no attention to the meaning of his style—his reverence for reason and for ordinary virtue—but had seized upon the revelation of the Unconscious as if it were the key to the whole of life. Reich, similarly, believed in the self-regulation of the organism. But by regulation he meant its harmony in a world which included rationality and duty. Just so, the character of Neill was not formed in a Summerhillian universe, but in a difficult world containing both traditional and revolutionary values. This world is present at Summerhill in the person of Neill, which is to say that many of its values are present by active demonstration, though they may not be much spoken of: values of rectitude, courage, patience, duty, pragmatic common sense. These are much in evidence, too, in Neill's writing, which helps to account, I think, for its popularity in this country, surfeited as we are with the voiceless "objectivity" of our hordes of Experts. If some few of Neill's disciples have minimized these things, it is because they have seized impatiently upon certain insights, namely, those which justify their own anger at a world that has injured them.

Summerhill is our chief point of reference, too, when the question of compulsory attendance comes up. This is an issue much discussed by libertarian teachers, and is one that will become important on a larger scale if the present liberalizing tendency in education should ever really alter our public schools. Should we compel attendance, or not? Neill tells us that at Summerhill the children are in no way pressured into attending classes. Unfortunately he does not tell us enough about what they do in the meantime. Some few purists that I have observed have bent over backwards on this issue, creating a kind of vacuum between themselves and their students in order to give the students' volition enough room to mature. This, it seems to me, is an error. It arises, in good part, from posing the problem in terms of attendance and compulsion.

But the whole issue, as we know it in this country, testifies to a really peculiar anxiety and lack of faith on the part of adults. Would children really abandon school if they were no longer compelled to attend? Or, more properly, would the acquisition of skills and knowledge and the participation in large-scale social life with their peers suddenly lose all attractiveness? The idea of *school*—not perhaps in its present bureaucratized form—is one of the most powerful social inventions that we possess. It rests squarely on the deepest of necessities and draws on motives we could not disavow even if we wished to. Teaching is one of the few natural functions of adults. Vis-à-vis the young, we simply cannot escape it. Too, our legitimate demand of the young—that in one style or another they be worthy inheritors of our world—is deeply respected by the young themselves. They form their notions of selfhood, individual pride, citizenship, etc., in precisely the terms that we put forward, converting our demands into goals and even into ideas of glory. I cannot believe all this is so feeble that we need to rest the function of education upon acts of compulsion, with all the damage this entails.

If compulsion is damaging and unwise, its antithesis—a vacuum of free choice—is unreal. And in fact we cannot deal with the problem in these terms, for the real question is not, What shall we do about classes? but, What shall we do about our relationships with the young? How shall we deepen them, enliven them, make them freer, more amiable, and at the same time more serious? How shall we broaden the area of mutual experience? If these things can be done, the question of school attendance, or classroom attendance, will take a simpler and more logical form, will lie closer to the fact that classroom instruction is, after all, a *method* (one among many) and deserves to be criticized in terms of its efficiency. It is not the be-all and end-all of a child's existence. Let me put this in terms of our experience at the First Street School.

It was not the case that there was a lesson available and that José, for example, was free to go or not to go. The first facts were otherwise. By first facts I mean the context within which the possibility of *any* lesson unavoidably arose.

1) He was thirteen years old and had behind him six years of the most abysmal failure. He did his best to hide his mortification, but it was obvious that he suffered because of his inability to learn. He was afraid to make another attempt, and at the same time, he wanted to.

2) We established a relationship. This was not difficult, for I liked him, though liking him would not have been essential. We spent several weeks getting to know each other, roughly three hours a day of conversations, games in the gym, outings, etc. We lived in the same neighborhood and saw each other on the streets. He knew me as George, not as "teacher."

3) He understood immediately that our school was different, that the teachers were present for reasons of their own and that the kind of concern they evinced was unusual, for there were no progress reports, or teacher ratings, or supervisors. Yet this concern, which appeared so unusual in a school setting, was identical with the everyday concern of his relatives and grown-up neighbors, who often asked him about his schoolwork and were obviously serious when they expressed their hopes for his future.

4) He understood that I had interests of my own, a life of my own that could not be defined by the word "teacher." And he knew that he, though not a large part of my life, was nevertheless a part of it.

Now given this background, what must José have thought about my wanting to teach him to read? For I did want to, and I made no bones about it. He saw that I considered it far more important than many of the fleeting feelings he expressed or exhibited.

The fact is, he took it for granted. It was the right and proper relationship, not of teacher and student, but of adult and child, for his relatives wanted him to read, and so did his neighbors; and if it were not for the dreadful pressures of life in the slums, among which are the public institutions and the general hatred thereof, many of them could have taught him. But the idea occurred to no one, least of all José.

And so I did not wait for José to decide for himself. When I thought the time was ripe, I insisted that we begin our lessons. My insistence carried a great deal of weight with him, since for reasons of his own he respected me. Too, his volition, in any event, could arise only from a background in which I myself already figured, with my own interests and my own manifestation of an adult concern he was accustomed to everywhere but in school. He did *not* feel that his own motives were no concern of mine. No child feels this. This belongs to the hang-ups of adolescence and the neuroses of the hippies. To a child, the motives of adults belong quite simply to the environment. They are like icebergs or attractive islands: one navigates between or heads straight for them. The child's own motives are similarly projected outward; they become occasions for dissimulation or closer contact. It is because of this that both affection and straight-out conflict come so easily. They come inevitably, and they belong, both together, to the teaching-learning experience.

My own demands, then, were an important part of José's experience. They were not simply the demands of a teacher, nor of an adult, but belonged to my own way of caring about José. And he sensed this. There was something he prized in the fact that I made demands on him. This became all the more evident once he realized that I wasn't simply processing him, that is, grading, measuring, etc. And when he learned that he *could* refuse—could refuse altogether, could terminate the lesson, could change its direction, could insist on something else—our mutual interest in his development was taken quite for granted. We became collaborators in the business of life.

Obviously, if I had tried to compel him, none of this would have been possible. And if I had made no demand—had simply waited for him to come to class—I would in some sense have been false to my own motives, my own engagement in the life of the school and the community. In his eyes I would have lost immediacy, would have lost reality, as it were, for I would have seemed more and more like *just* a teacher. What he prized, after all, was this: *that an adult with a life of his own, was willing to teach him.* [Italics added.]

How odd it is to have to say this! What a vast perversion of the natural relations of children and adults has been worked by our bureaucratized system of public education! It was important to José that I was not just a teacher, but a writer as well, that I was interested in painting and had friends who were artists, that I took part in civil rights demonstrations. To the extent that he sensed my life stretching out beyond him into (for him) the unknown, my meaning as an adult was enhanced, and the things I already knew and might teach him gained the luster they really possess in life. This is true for every teacher, every student. No teacher is just a teacher, no student just a student. The life meaning which joins them is the *sine qua non* for the process of education, yet precisely this is destroyed in the public schools because everything is standardized and the persons are made to vanish into their roles. This is exactly Sartre's definition of inauthenticity. I am reminded here, too, of how often John Dewey and, in our own time, Paul Goodman and Elliott Shapiro have urged the direct use of the community. The world *as it exists* is what the young are hungry for; and we give them road maps, mere diagrams of the world at a distance.

* * *

I have mentioned how important we found the writings of A. S. Neill and the example of his Summerhill School in England. There was another school, too, whose history meant much to us, and of whose existence not many persons have been aware. This was the free school that Leo Tolstoy set up for the peasant children of his own estate, Yásnaya Polyána. He himself taught in the school for three years, and wrote brilliantly of it in a short-lived magazine published at his own expense. These writings—out of print for decades—have been reissued recently by the University of Chicago Press (*Tolstoy on Education*).

In moral and religious matters, Tolstoy at that time was quite conventional (though one can hardly call the earnestness of his beliefs conventional); otherwise he was iconoclastic, a good century ahead of his time, and very often expressed thoughts and described practices identical with those of A. S. Neill. He developed themes, too, that we find again in the pages of John Dewey, stressing the experimental nature of education, its tendency toward social equality, the persisting need to reexamine the past so as to escape the dead hand of authority, and the importance of bringing the school into active relations with the life of the times. The choicest things in these essays, however, are Tolstoy's descriptions of the children responding to the freedom, or "the free order" (as he calls it), of their school. These descriptions are so vivid and alive, and are so instructive, that I would, if I could, quote the entire book, though I know that by now many persons must have obtained the new edition. What these pictures from life bring home to us is the actual anatomy of inborn human faculties, and how they flower under conditions that support their growth. And how different this is from the writings of our own educational researchers, who though they stress the importance of intrinsic motives and patterned growth, write as if they had no faith whatsoever in the existence of these things, placing their reliance, as ever, on the opinions and orders of a handful of administrators!

Since the descriptions I have just mentioned are too lengthy to quote, and are too delicious to summarize, let me give a few extracts from other sections that will indicate the nature of the school and its bearing on present-day libertarian practice.

> In spite of the preponderating influence of the teacher, the pupil has always had the right not to come to school, or, having come, not to listen to the teacher. The teacher has had the right not to admit a pupil, and has had the possibility of bringing to bear all the force of his influence on the majority of pupils. . . . The farther the pupils proceed, the more the instruction branches out and the more necessary does order become. For this reason, in the normal non-compulsory development of the school, the more the pupils become educated, the fitter they become for order,

From: The Lives of Children 33

and the more strongly they themselves feel the need for order. . . . Now we have pupils in the first class, who themselves demand that the programme be adhered to, who are dissatisfied when they are disturbed in their lessons, and who constantly drive out the little ones who run in to them. In my opinion this external disorder is useful and not to be replaced by anything else, however strange and inconvenient it may be for the teacher. I shall often have occasion to speak of the advantages of this system, and now I will say only this much about the reputed inconveniences: First, this disorder, or free order, is terrible to us only because we are accustomed to something quite different, in which we have been educated. Secondly, in this case, as in many similar cases, force is used only through haste and through insufficient respect for human nature. We think that the disorder is growing greater and greater, and that there are no limits to it,—we think that there is no other means of stopping it but by the use of force,—whereas we only need to wait a little, and the disorder (or animation) calms down naturally by itself, growing into a much better and more permanent order than what we have created.

How often have I seen children fighting, when the teacher would rush up to take them apart, which would only make the separated enemies look awry at each other, and would not keep them, even in the presence of a stern teacher, from rushing later against each other in order to inflict a more painful kick! How often do I see every day some Kiryúshka, with set teeth, fly at Taráska, pull his hair, knock him down, and, if it costs him his life, try to maim his enemy,—and not a minute passes before Taráska laughs underneath Kiryúshka,—it is so much easier personally to square up accounts; in less than five minutes both become friends and sit down near each other.

The parents' dissatisfaction with the absence of corporal punishment and order at the school has now almost entirely disappeared. I have often had occasion to observe the perplexity of a father, when, coming to the school for his boy, he saw the pupils running about, making a hubbub, and tussling with each other. He is convinced that naughtiness is detrimental, and yet he believes that we teach well, and he is at a loss to combine the two.

The two lower classes meet in one room, while the advanced class goes to the next. The teacher comes, and, in the lowest class, all surround him at the board, or on the benches, or sit or lie on the table about the teacher or one of the reading boys. If it is a writing lesson, they seat themselves in a more orderly way, but they keep getting up, in order to look at the copy-books of the others, and to show theirs to the teacher.

According to the program, there are to be four lessons before noon, but there sometimes are only three or two, and sometimes there are entirely different subjects. The teacher may begin with arithmetic and pass over to geometry, or he may start on sacred history, and end up with grammar. At times the teacher and pupils are so carried away, that, instead of one hour, the class lasts three hours. Sometimes the pupils themselves cry: "More, more!" and scold those who are tired of the subject: "If you are tired, go to the babies!"

All the evening lessons, especially the first, have a peculiar character of calm, dreaminess, and poetry, differing in this from the morning classes. You come to the school at fall of day: no lights are seen in the windows; it is almost quiet, and only tracks of snow on the staircase, freshly carried in, a weak din and rustling behind the door, and some urchin clattering on the staircase, taking two steps at a time and holding on to the balustrade, prove that the pupils are at school.

Walk into the room! It is almost dark behind the frozen windows; the best pupils are jammed toward the teacher by the rest of the children, and, turning up their little heads, are looking straight into the teacher's mouth. The independent manorial girl is always sitting with a careworn face on the high table, and, it seems, is swallowing every word; the poorer pupils, the small fry, sit farther away: they listen attentively, even austerely; they behave just like the big boys, but, in spite of their attention, we know that they will not tell a thing, even though they may remember some.

Some press down on other people's shoulders, and others stand up on the table. Occasionally one pushes his way into the crowd, where he busies himself drawing some figures with his nail on somebody's back. It is not often that one will look back at you. When a new story is being told, all listen in dead silence; when there is a repetition, ambitious voices are heard now and then, being unable to keep from helping the teacher out. Still, if there is an old story which they like, they ask the teacher to repeat it in his own words, and then they do not allow any one to interrupt him.

"What is the matter with you? Can't you hold in? Keep quiet!" they will call out to a forward boy.

It pains them to hear the character and the artistic quality of the teacher's story interrupted. Of late it has been the story of Christ's life. They every time asked to have it all told to them. If the whole story is not told to them, they themselves supply their favourite ending,—the history of Peter's denying Christ, and of the Saviour's passion.

You would think all are dead: there is no stir,—can they be asleep? You walk up to them in the semi-darkness and look into the face of some little fellow,—he is sitting, his eyes staring at the teacher, frowning from close attention, and for the tenth time brushing away the arm of his companion, which is pressing down on his shoulder. You tickle his neck,—he does not even smile; he only bends his head, as though to drive away a fly, and again abandons himself to the mysterious and poetical story, how the veil of the church was rent and it grew dark upon earth,—and he has a mingled sensation of dread and joy.

Now the teacher is through with his story, and all rise from their seats, and, crowding around their teacher, try to outcry each other in their attempt to tell what they have retained. There is a terrible hubbub,—the teacher barely can follow them all. Those who are forbidden to tell anything, the teacher being sure that they know it all, are not satisfied: they approach the other teacher; and if he is not there, they importune a companion, a stranger, even the keeper of the fires, or walk from corner to corner by twos and by threes, begging everybody to listen to them. It is rare for one to tell at a time. They themselves divide up in groups, those of equal strength keeping together, and begin to tell, encouraging and correcting each other, and waiting for their turns. "Come, let us take it together," says one to another, but the one who is addressed knows that he can't keep up with him, and so sends him to another. As soon as they have had their say and have quieted down, lights are brought, and a different mood comes over the boys.

At times, when the classes are uninteresting, and there have been many of them (we often have seven long hours a day), and the children are tired, or before the holidays, when the ovens at home are prepared for a hot bath, two or three boys will suddenly rush into the room during the second or third afternoon class-hour, and will hurriedly pick out their caps.

"What's up?"
"Going home."
"And the studies? There is to be singing yet!"
"The boys say they are going home," says one, slipping away with his cap.
"Who says so?"
"The boys are gone!"
"How is that?" asks the perplexed teacher who has prepared his lesson. "Stay!"

But another boy runs into the room, with an excited and perplexed face.
"What are you staying here for?" he angrily attacks the one held back, who, in indecision, pushes the cotton batting back into his cap. "The boys are way down there,—I guess as far as the smithy."
"Have they gone?"
"They have."

And both run away, calling from behind the door: "Good-bye, Iván Ivánovich!"

Who are the boys that decided to go home, and how did they decide it? God knows. You will never find out who decided it. They did not take counsel, did not conspire, but simply, some boys wanted to go home, "The boys are going!"—and their feet rattle down-stairs, and one rolls down the steps in catlike form, and, leaping and tumbling in the snow, running a race with each other along the narrow path, the children bolt for home.

Such occurrences take place once or twice a week. It is aggravating and disagreeable for the teacher,—who will not admit that? But who will not admit, at the same time, that, on account of one such an occurrence, the five, six, and even seven lessons a day for each class, which are, of their own accord and with pleasure, attended by the pupils, receive a so much greater significance? . . . Their continued willingness to come to school, in spite of the liberty granted them, does not, I think, by any means prove the especial qualities of the Yásnaya Polyána school,—I believe that the same would be repeated in the majority of schools, and that the desire to study is so strong in children that, in order to satisfy their desire, they will submit to many hard conditions and will forgive many defects.

Many times, reading the pages of Tolstoy, I have been struck by the differences between the peasant children and some of ours. What would those sturdy lads have thought of Julio, Vicente, and Stanley, who could not speak to adults at all—let alone figures of authority—without cringing or blustering? The young peasants were children of oppression. We find phrases of Tolstoy's—"a fine musician," "a remarkable mathematician," "the correctness of his poetical conceptions"—and realize that these richly endowed children are destined for the fields and pantries, and we sense the revolution in the non-too-distant future. Yet it seems to me that some of the children at First Street suffered an even greater deprivation, a disorder and impoverishment that struck at the very roots of life. In the place of fields and growing things, animals, trees, weather, the sky, they knew only the nerve-shattering noises of the streets, the dingy buildings, the crowded sidewalks, the starless gray pall that hangs over our heads where the sky used to be. Where the peasant children acquired the skills of farming and carpentry and dozens of other necessary occupations, and therefore knew that they were indeed necessary persons, ours had acquired nothing and could do nothing, and did not at all feel necessary to the inner life of labor that sustains a country. They were, and felt, superfluous. At the same time, they were battered and invaded from all sides. Store windows, billboards, posters—all tempted them to want things and urged them to buy. Television took the place of family voices at night. Their parents were distraught. There was nowhere to go. The streets were hostile and confining. The hallways smelled of piss and wine. It was little wonder that our older pupils were mistrustful and violent, impatient, resentful, undeveloped. It *was* a wonder —an unending one—that they had preserved so much of the vitality of youth, and that they responded so quickly to radical changes in their environment.

Before opening his school as Yásnaya Polyána, Tolstoy had toured schools in France, Germany, and England, and had familiarized himself with the growing literature on education. His critique of prevailing customs appeared in the earliest issues of the magazine, together with his own closely reasoned theories of education, of which not the least important feature was that they were based as much upon considerations of morality as upon the nature of the process of learning. The relation between his own practice and this earlier critique can be seen in such observations as these:

> School is established, not in order that it should be convenient for the children to study, but that the teachers should be able to teach in comfort. The children's conversation, motion, and merriment, which are their necessary conditions of study, are not convenient for the teacher, and so in the schools—which are built on the plan of prisons—questions, conversation, and motion are prohibited. . . . Schools which are established from above and by force are not a shepherd for the flock, but a flock for the shepherd.

> Instead of convincing themselves that in order to act successfully on a certain object, it is necessary to study it (in education this object is the

free child), they want to teach just as they know how, as they think best, and in case of failure they want to change, not the manner of their teaching, but the nature of the child itself. From this attitude have sprung and even now spring (Pestalozzi) such systems as would allow to *mécaniser l'instruction,*—that eternal tendency of pedagogy to arrange matters in such a way that, no matter who the teacher and who the pupil may be, the method should remain one and the same.

I have quoted chiefly the remarks that bear upon the relations of teachers and pupils. Tolstoy experimented considerably with curriculum and methods of teaching. If these experiments seem less relevant to our situation today, it is because we have already invested immense labors of research in these matters. We are not at a loss for structured curriculum, and there is no lack of variety and refinement in materials and methods. We lack only the essentials: a working relationship between pupils and teachers, a living bond between school and community.

One last observation of Tolstoy's is worth stressing here—since America is uniquely cursed with a reading problem—and this is that learning to read is not difficult, but easy. What is needed is to remove the obstacles that prevent reading from assuming its inherent relationship with speech, and cease the practices that destroy the motivation which for this subject is ordinarily strong and deep. In November of 1967, in an address to the Manhattan Borough President's hearing on decentralization, Paul Goodman presented the case for mini-schools and based much of his argument upon a brilliant summation of the conditions that are necessary if a child is to learn to read. The public schools, he pointed out, systematically destroy these requisites.

> According to some neurophysiologists, given the exposure to written code in modern urban and suburban conditions, any emotionally normal child in middle-class surroundings will spontaneously learn to read by age nine, just as he learned to speak by age three. It is impossible for him not to pick up the code unless he is systematically interrupted and discouraged. . . .

Goodman's speech first appeared in the *Chelsea Clinton News*. It attracted letters of approbation, but also—from teachers and principals—expressions of disapproval. They could not believe that a child, without instruction, could do so much. Nor could they believe that learning to read is a far easier task than learning to speak. Tolstoy, not once but many times, records conversations such as these:

> I asked him [a fourteen-year-old peasant boy] syllabication and he knew it; I made him read, and he read without spelling out, although he did not believe he could do it.
> "Where did you study?"
> "In the summer I was with a fellow shepherd; he knew, and he taught me to read."

"Have you an ABC book?"
"Yes."
"Where did you get it?"
"I bought it."
"How long have you been studying?"
"During the summer: I studied whenever he showed me in the field."

Again:

> ... a boy ten years of age once brought his brother to me. This boy, seven years old, read well, and had learned to do so from his brother during the evenings of one winter. I know many such examples, and whoever wants to look for them among the masses will find very many such cases.

At his own school Tolstoy made use of the mutual teaching that works such wonders among children. (As Joseph Featherstone tells us of the liberalized public schools of England: "At first it is hard to say just how they do learn reading, since there are no separate subjects. A part of the answer slowly becomes clear, and it surprises American visitors used to thinking of the teacher as the generating force of education: children learn from each other.") Other methods used were group reading, memorizing of poems and prayers, and individual, undirected work. Both the phonic and the Look-Say techniques played their part. Everything was based, however, on the first of the four methods Tolstoy describes:

> The *first*, in use by the mothers of the whole world, is not a scholastic, but a domestic method. It consists in the pupil's coming and asking to read with the teacher, whereupon the teacher reads, guiding his every syllable and the combination of syllables,—the very first rational and immutable method, which the pupil is the first to demand, and upon which the teacher involuntarily hits. In spite of all the means which are supposed to mechanize instruction and presumably facilitate the work of the teacher with a large number of pupils, this method will always remain the best and the only one for teaching people to read, and to read fluently.

JONATHAN KOZOL
Free Schools

*Free School as a Term Meaning
Too Many Different Things: What
Other People Mean—What I Mean—
What I Do Not Mean*

The term "Free School" is used very often, in a cheerful but unthinking way, to mean entirely different kinds of things and to define the dreams and yearnings of entirely disparate and even antagonistic individuals and groups. It is honest, then, to say, right from the start, that I am speaking mainly of one type of Free School and that many of the ventures which go under the name of Free School will not be likely to find much of their own experience reflected here.

At one end of the spectrum, there is the large, public-school-connected, neighborhood-created, and politically controversial operation best exemplified perhaps by I.S. 201, in its initial phase, or later by Ocean Hill-Brownsville in New York. Somewhat smaller, but still involving some of the same factors, and still tied in with the public-education apparatus, is the Morgan School in Washington, D.C. At the opposite extreme is a rather familiar type of physically isolated, politically noncontroversial, and generally all-white, high-tuition Free School. This kind of school is often tied in with a commune or with what is described as an "intentional community," attracts people frequently who, if not rich, have parents who are wealthy, and is often associated with a certain kind of media-promoted counterculture.

Neither of the two descriptions just preceding would apply directly to the kind of Free School I have tended to be most intensively involved

From *Free Schools* by Jonathan Kozol. Copyright © 1972 by Jonathan Kozol. Reprinted by permission of the publisher, Houghton Mifflin Company.

with, though certainly I have been a great deal closer to the first than to the second. There is also a considerable difference in the way I feel about the two. The large, political, and public-school-associated ventures like Ocean Hill-Brownsville are, in my opinion, brave, significant, and in many ways heroic struggles for survival on the part of those who constitute the most despised and brutalized and properly embittered victims of North American racism and class exploitation. While these are not the kinds of schools that I am writing about here, they seem to me to be of vast importance, and I look upon the people who are active in them with immense respect.

The other end of the spectrum does not seem to me to be especially courageous or heroic. In certain ways it appears to me to be a dangerous and disheartening phenomenon—the radical version of benign neglect. I know, of course, that very persuasive arguments can be presented for the idea of escaping from the turmoil and the human desperation of the cities, and for finding a place of physical isolation in the mountains of Vermont or in the hills of Southern California. Like many people here in Boston and New York, I have often felt the urge to run away, especially when I see a picture or read something in a magazine about these pastoral and isolated Free Schools in their gentle and attractive settings of hillside, farmland, and warm country meadow. When I am the most weary, the inclination to escape is almost overwhelming.

Despite this inclination, which I feel so often, I believe we have an obligation to stay here and fight these battles and work out these problems in the cities, where there is the greatest need, and where, moreover, we cannot so easily be led into a mood of falsified euphoria. If a man should feel, as many people do, that whites should not be working in black neighborhoods, then there are plenty of poor white neighborhoods in major cities, or neighborhoods of the marginal lower-middle class along the edges of the major cities, as well as in several of the rural neighborhoods of Appalachia and the Deep South and Southwest, areas of need, of pain and devastation—in which we might establish roots and settle down to try to build our Free Schools and to develop those communities of struggle which so frequently grow up around them. I know it is very appealing, and for people who are weary from a long, long period of fruitless struggle and rebellion, it is almost irresistible to get away from everything. I don't believe, however, that we should give in to this yearning, even if it is very appealing and even if we are very, very weary. In any case, I am addressing this book primarily to those who do not plan to run away.

There is one point about the exodus of rich people to the woods and hills which is, to me, particularly disturbing. Some of the most conscientious and reflective of the people in the upper-class Free Schools will often seek to justify their manner of escape by pointing out that they, and their young children with them, have in a sense "retired" from the

North American system as a whole, and especially from its agencies of devastation, power, and oppression. Though earnestly presented, this argument does not seem honest. Whether they like it or not, or whether they wish to speak of it or not, the beautiful children of the rich and powerful within this nation are going to be condemned to wield that power also. This power, which will be theirs if they are cognizant of it, and even if they aren't, will be the power to affect the lives of millions of poor men and women in this nation, to do so often in the gravest ways, often indeed to grant or to deny life to these people. It will be the power, as well, to influence the lives of several hundred million people who are now subject to North American domination in far distant lands. Even in the idealistic ritual of formal abdication of that power, as, for example, by going out into the isolated hills of western Massachusetts or into the mountains of Vermont to start a Free School, they will still be profiting from the consequences of that power and from the direct profits and extractions of a structure of oppression.

Free Schools, then, cannot, with sanity, with candor, or with truth, endeavor to exist within a moral vacuum. However far the journey and however many turnpike tolls we pay, however high the spruce or pine that grow around the sunny meadows in which we live and dream and seek to educate our children, it is still one nation. It is not one thing in Lebanon, New Hampshire: one thing in the heart of Harlem. No more is it one thing in Roxbury or Watts, one thing in Williamsburg or Canyon, California. The passive, tranquil, and protected lives white people lead depend on strongly armed police, well-demarcated ghettos. While children starve and others walk the city streets in fear on Monday afternoon, the privileged young people in the Free Schools of Vermont shuttle their handlooms back and forth and speak of love and of "organic processes." They do "their thing." Their thing is sun and good food and fresh water and good doctors and delightful, old, and battered eighteenth-century houses, and a box of baby turtles; somebody else's thing may be starvation, broken glass, unheated rooms, and rats inside the bed with newborn children. The beautiful children do not *wish* cold rooms or broken glass, starvation, rats, or fear for anybody; nor will they stake their lives, or put their bodies on the line, or interrupt one hour of the sunlit morning, or sacrifice one moment of the golden afternoon, to take a hand in altering the unjust terms of a society in which these things are possible.

I know that I will antagonize many people by the tenor of these statements; yet I believe them deeply and cannot keep faith with the people I respect, and who show loyalty to me, if I put forward a piece of writing of this kind and do not say these things. In my belief, an isolated upper-class Free School for the children of the white and rich within a land like the United States and in a time of torment such as 1972 is a great deal too much like a sandbox for the children of the S.S. guards at

Auschwitz. If today in our history books, or in our common conversation, we were to hear of a network of exquisite, idealistic little country schools operated with a large degree of personal freedom, but within the bounds of ideological isolation, in the beautiful sloping woodlands outside of Munich and Berlin in 1939 or 1940, and if we were to read or to be told that those who ran these schools were operating by all innovative methods and enlightened notions and that they had above their desks or on their walls large poster-photographs of people like Maria Montessori and Tolstoi and Gandhi, and that they somehow kept beyond the notice of the Nazi government and of the military and of the police and S.S. guards, but kept right on somehow throughout the war with no experience of rage or need for intervention in the lives of those defined by the German press and media as less than human, but kept right on with water play and "innovative" games while smoke rose over Dachau . . . I think that we would look upon those people now as some very fine and terrifying breed of alienated human beings.

It is not a handsome or a comfortable parallel; yet, in my judgment it is not entirely different from the situation of a number of the country communes and the segregated Summerhills that we now see in certain sections of this nation. At best, these schools are obviating pain and etherizing evil; at worst, they constitute a registered escape valve for political rebellion. Least conscionable is when the people who are laboring and living in these schools describe themselves as revolutionaries. If this is revolution, then the men who have elected Richard Nixon do not have a lot to fear. They would do well in fact to subsidize these schools and to covertly channel resources to their benefactors and supporters, for they are an ideal drain on activism and the perfect way to sidetrack ethical men from dangerous behavior.

Hard Skills in General
White Anguish: Black Despair

In the preceding section I have taken an explicit and straightforward stand in direct opposition to a number of forms of pedagogic imposition which I consider innocent, naïve, or dangerous. This is a position which can lend itself to purposeful distortion on the part of those who are not sympathetic to the Free Schools in the first place and who might for this reason wish to drive a wedge within our ranks. It is important to me, therefore, to take pains to make my point of view more clear, less general and perhaps less subject to distortion.

The basic point that I am trying to establish in this book is the distinction between the life-style "revolution" of rich people, which transpires at all times within the safe and nonpolitical context of the white, the whimsical, the privileged, the not-in-need, and the real-life revolution of those who are in great pain or in grave danger—whether they might be black or white or Spanish-speaking—and who, as a consequence, are locked into a nonstop struggle for survival. The first pertains to individual transformations, better relations between those who are already given access to the proceeds of an unjust and unequal social order, a more inspiring and more meaningful experience of what life has to offer to those who have already all they need for physical health and for material well-being; the second, to matters of power, cash, oppression, exploitation, confrontation and control. I do not propose that serious young white men and women ought to abdicate their principles of personal and inward liberation in the face of middle-class traditions or conventional social expectations. I do propose, however, that the way to forge or to empower an important, ethical or political upheaval in the consciousness of those who are the mothers, fathers, sisters, brothers of poor children is not through imposition but through the slow and gradual process of reciprocal instruction.

It is inevitable, being a college-educated white man, as I am, with many of the appropriate labels and appropriate credentials, that I would be somewhat less reticent and more articulate here in pointing to the impositions of the white men and white women like myself than to the impositions that are coming from the opposite direction. I am not certain if it is for this reason or some other; I do know that I tend to side more frequently against some of the views and impositions of the young white teachers than against those of the parents of the black and Spanish children. Whatever the bias that I bring to bear, it is important in this section to attempt to pin down two or three of the essential issues which appear to lie beneath the surface in these kinds of conflicts.

There is, to begin with, the very plain and simple truth that a big portion of the anti-skill, anti-credential confidence of most white people in the counterculture is not an authentic and by no means a risk-taking confidence inasmuch as it exists within a context of the most inexorable and least destructible protections. It is only the child of the owner of the biggest shoe store in New Jersey who thinks it is radical to go in bare feet in the streets of Harlem. To the poor, who live within those streets of broken glass and in those canyons of cracked asphalt and concrete, it is not radical to cut your feet on glass or freeze your feet in slush and snow; it is (a) mockery, (b) satire, (c) madness.

Too often, the young white woman or young white man that I have in mind refuses to recognize the very great degree to which his own, or her own, sense of personal rebellion or of "life-style" resistance is built upon the deep-down confidence, the deep-down knowledge and unquestioned certitude that, in one hour or in one afternoon, she could put on her shoes and cut her hair, fish out an old but still familiar piece of plastic from her pocketbook or wallet, go to Brattle Street or go to Bonwit Teller, buy new clothes, and walk into a brand-new job. Most of the young white people that I know do not like to let on that they have, in fact, this sense of intellectual and financial back-up. The parents of poor children, however, recognize this sort of thing quite clearly; they also recognize, and with equal clarity, (a) that their children do not have protection of this kind, (b) that, without a certain degree of skillful and aggressive adaptation to the present conditions of the system they are fighting, they will simply not survive.

The invocations to risk-taking actions and to anti-skill, anti-curricular rebellion which so many of these white people often eloquently put forth would be more powerful and would, I think, be infinitely more persuasive and more credible if there were something more of perseverance and of sustained commitment offered by those who are speaking in this fashion. It is unfortunate that this is seldom the real case. Indeed, one of the most familiar characteristics of the kinds of people I now have in mind is the ephemeral quality of their conviction and the reiterated sequence of arrival, verbal imposition, conflict and departure. It is difficult for many of the black, the Spanish-speaking or the white working-class people that I know, in face of new arrivals from the outside world, to lose sight of the quite remarkable numbers of such men and women who arrive and go, appear and disappear, with every season. There is a pattern that the mothers and the fathers have identified by now and speak of with a sense of lyrical recognition: "They arrive with the coming of the birds and with the first warmth of the sun in the last weeks of April. They are gone by the falling of the leaves in late September."

It is, in part, for reasons of this kind that I would wish to urge upon my colleagues, allies and co-workers that we be rather cautious and, if it is in our power also, something less than absolute and dictatorial in the determination to impose our newest and most strident ideologies upon the mothers and the fathers of the children of poor people. Those who quote most frequently from Ivan Illich in the presence of the poor are inevitably the first ones to go back to Harvard to complete their Ph.D. It is, in all likelihood, for reasons of this kind that serious black leaders, and sophisticated leaders in Puerto Rican neighborhoods and poor white neighborhoods as well, now stipulate that teachers, volunteers, outsiders, of whatever point of view, must demonstrate something more than ordinary sticking power, of long-term perseverance and of sustained affiliation, before they are invited to participate in any serious respect within the major processes of education, policy-making, and decision.

Freire speaks, in several ways and at a number of points within his work, of the pedagogic obligation for *immersion in the situation of the victim*, as opposed to an undangerous or cost-free location close to, but above. I drive one evening, with one of the more influential leaders of the counterculture, through some of the roughest and most desperate neighborhoods of Roxbury. He looks at the streets, and he looks at the houses, and he looks at all the devastated empty lots; he shakes his head, and he says: "Gee whiz—a couple of gallons of paint would sure make a big difference." Two weeks later he is back in Colorado or New Mexico, leading another seminar on "pedagogic innovation."

Hundreds of young white people every year come into the neighborhood with more or less the same benign, well-meaning but preposterous point of view. I do not object if I appear, by statements of this kind, to take the role of one who knows what some of my co-workers do not know; I do, in fact, base the views and judgments which are offered in this book upon specific truth and on first-person witness. I do not intend to hide behind an objectivity to which I have no claim. Several of the finest Free Schools in the nation, such as Highland Park, require that teachers live within the neighborhood in which the school is situated. I do not know if this is a realistic stipulation in all cases; there may be times or places where it just would not be possible. I do know that something in the nature of a long-term, steadfast, physical immersion in the material conditions of the neighborhood in which the Free School stands is one very good and sane and sober way to guard against the fatuous idea that two gallons, or two thousand gallons, of bright paint would make a serious difference in a neighborhood of men and women who are starving. It is also, perhaps, the only way by which to guarantee that each of our perceptions, insights, and ideas will be constructed on the recognition of real needs—not those which are abstracted by the lecture hall or neutralized by seminars and convocations.

The hard, immediate and specific sense of panic which derives from social insult, sickness, hunger, physical alarm, the scream of the siren, and the blue light spinning in the morning sky, the desperation of the fourteen-year-old mother in the back-street clinic of a miserable northern city slum—these are the ordinary metaphors of need and pain which must at all times govern the decisions and intentions of a strong, realistic, unromantic urban Free School in the decade of the 1970's. In this neighborhood, here in the South End of Boston, there is one family of three children and their mother whom I have known now for six years; mother and children must sustain themselves upon an annual income of three thousand dollars. Another family to which my wife and I are drawn, through friendships with two of the older children, has had to get through several twelve-month periods in the past few years on eighteen hundred dollars; there are *ten children* in this family. Men and women who are locked into such lives as these cannot be expected to look without uneasiness or even without considerable alarm at those who tell them that their children do not need competitive skills, do not need math, do not need English, do not need to find out how to psych out a complex and difficult exam, do not need universities, do not need money, do not need ugly, wicked, contaminated, middle-class "success." The issue for the children that I have in mind is not success. It is survival.

The lives of children in the immediate neighborhood of Boston in which I now live constitute, by any index and by all criteria that any reasonable man might have in mind, medical, economic and educational disaster areas. Black children in this neighborhood of Boston, with basic competence the same as that of any child in the midst of North Dakota or in the wheatfields of Nebraska, are, statistically, by fifth-grade level, at least one year behind their white suburban counterparts in basic coding and decoding skills like math and reading; by seventh-grade level, two years behind; by ninth-grade level, four years; by twelfth-grade level (if they ever get there), four or five years. Statistics for the Puerto Rican children in this neighborhood of Boston are, if possible, still worse than those for blacks. Ninety percent of the Puerto Rican kids in public school in Boston drop out of school before they get into the tenth grade. In a Puerto Rican population of approximately forty thousand people, there are at this writing fewer than seventy children in *all levels* of the public high schools. The odds these children face, first on surviving the attrition rate between first grade and twelfth grade, then on being able to go on to higher education, are approximately one-twentieth the odds of kids in ordinary white suburban schools, one-thirtieth the odds of kids in places such as Evanston and Greenwich, one-fiftieth the odds of kids who go to places like St. Paul's and Exeter and Groton.

The medical odds with which the children in these neighborhoods must live are even more alarming. Black children in the United States have approximately twice the chance of dying in the first twelve months of life as white children born in the same section of the nation on the same day. The national average is twenty infant deaths per thousand. In white suburban neighborhoods, the figure is much closer to fifteen. In black communities like Harlem, Watts, Newark, the figure seldom runs lower than thirty or thirty-five, and in some areas it runs as high as fifty. It is commonly assumed that the most serious instances of catastrophic health conditions, of deficient diet and of inadequate medical service are to be found within the rural South. In the event that we feel smug, however, in our northern point of view, Dr. H. Jack Geigar of Tufts-New England Medical Center points out that there are a number of northern ghetto census tracts in the United States in which the infant-mortality rate exceeds *one hundred deaths* for every thousand children. This figure transcends the curse visited by the Hebrew God upon the land of Egypt in the book of Exodus.

It is desperately important, in my own belief, that those of us who join together to create and nourish a community of conscience in the concrete substance of a small and passionate and dedicated Free School should understand, deep in our heart and soul, before we start, the grave, immoderate and inescapable dimensions of the human context of our struggle and our labor. For poor people in the United States the risk of dying prior to age thirty-five is four times the average for the nation as a whole. In certain areas of the Deep South, the death rate for black women in the act of giving birth is now six times the rate for whites. Ten to fifteen thousand people, mainly black and Puerto Rican, die an unnecessary death each year in New York City; statistically, they fall into the category called "excess mortality." The figure for newborn infants nationwide is estimated to be as high as forty thousand. The heaviest concentrations of these infant deaths are in the rural slums of the Deep South and in the northern ghetto. These forty thousand children are the victims of gross medical injustice, both created and maintained by the surrounding white and middle-class population which derives direct and measurable advantage from the unjust allocation of available resources. There is no way to classify these children other than as the victims of social, professional and institutional murder.

Those children who survive the hour of their imperfect birth incur a number of equally formidable dangers in the first few years of life. The medical consequences of lead poison from the lead paint used in much of Boston's worst slum housing are now gradually coming to the attention of the parents and community leaders in these neighborhoods. The crumbling plaster is covered with sweet-tasting chips of lead paint that poor children eat or chew as it flakes off the walls. The lead paint poisons the brain cells of young children. Infants die, are paralyzed, undergo convulsions and sometimes grow blind if they chew it over a long period of time. The forces of the law in Boston do not compel a landlord to replace, repair or cover over the sweet-tasting crust of paint that paralyzes children. The law *does* allow a landlord to take action to evict a family if the mother or father misses one rent payment by as much as fifteen days. Even in those cases where the technicalities of the law might ordinarily be to the advantage of the black man or the black woman who is the tenant of the house in question, it is repeatedly proven to be the case that certain judges in this city, as in most others in the North with which I am familiar, will not seriously penalize or publicly embarrass those rich and powerful owners of slum properties who are their friends, the friends of politicians who appoint them, or, as in some instances that we have seen in Boston in the past two years, the major contributors to political campaigns.

It is in this context, then, that even the most highly "conscious" and politically sophisticated parents of poor children in such cities as my own draw back in hesitation, fear or anger at the often condescending if, in the long run, idealistic statements and intentions of those who attempt to tell them to forget about English syntax and the preparation for the Mathematics College Boards but send away for bean seeds and for organic food supplies and get into "group-talk" and "encounter." It seems to me that the parents are less backward and more realistic than some of their white co-workers are prepared to recognize. It seems to me that a tough, aggressive, skeptical and inventive "skill" like learning how to undermine and to attack a tough and racist and immensely difficult examination for the civil service, for City College or for Harvard Law School rings a good deal more of deep-down revolution than the hand-looms and the science gadgets and the gerbil cages that have come, in just five years, to constitute an innovative orthodoxy on a scale no less totalitarian than the old Scott, Foresman reader.

To plant a bean seed in a cut-down milk container and to call this "revolution" is to degrade and undermine the value of one of the sacred words. To show a poor black kid in East St. Louis or in Winston-Salem or in Chicago how to make end runs around the white man's college-entrance scores—while never believing that those scores are more than evil digits written on the sky—to do this, in my scale of values, is the starting point of an authentic revolution. It is not to imitate a confrontation, but to participate in one. It is not to speak of doing "our own thing," but rather to do one thing that really matters and can make a visible difference in the lives of our own brothers in the streets that stand about our school. Harlem does not need a new generation of radical basket weavers. It does need radical, strong, subversive, steadfast, skeptical, rage-minded, and power-wielding obstetricians, pediatricians, lab technicians, defense attorneys, building-code examiners, brain surgeons. Leather and wheat germ may appear to constitute a revolution in the confines of a far-removed and well-protected farm or isolated commune ten miles east of Santa Barbara or sixteen miles south of Santa Fe, but it does not do much good on Blue Hill Avenue in Boston on a Sunday evening if a man's pocket is empty and his child has a fever and the buses have stopped running.

There has to be a way to find pragmatic competence, internal strength and ethical passion all in the same process. This is the only kind of revolution that can possibly transform the lives of people in the land in which we live and in the time in which we are now living.

Permanent Struggle:
Location: Life Style: Confrontation:

Free Schools cannot function as life-giving and impassioned organizations if they do not have the means or will to generate a brilliant, strong, and self-renewing sense of permanent struggle. Many Free Schools that I know in Boston, and in some other areas such as New York City, begun in a state of mind which is white-hot, intense, determined, and inexorably involved with human struggle, derive from this their deepest energies, their deepest consciousness and their most solemn sense of good comradeship. Much of this consciousness, in my belief, comes from the sense of direct confrontation with the public sechools, as well as from the kinds of confrontations with municipal offices, the building code, the Fire Inspector, and the rest, that constitute a large part of the early struggle to establish the new venture. In particular, though, it is the sharp and recent memory of public school—the knowledge, vivid, strong and constantly renourished, of just how brutal, trivial and life-taking public school within a ghetto neighborhood can be. It does not require an incantation of the Summerhillian Gospel; neither does it ask the reading of Important Books on "serious social issues" to remind the mother of a six-year-old black child in the South End of this city to look into her child's eyes at four o'clock when he comes home from school and see the fire and the bitterness burning there.

Then, too, the visits that a worried mother makes to the principal's office at the local public school, the defensive statistics and the falsified sense of amicable good will in the deceitful eyes of principal or guidance counselor or schoolteacher, the stale air and the hypocritical symbols, pledge of flag and words of anthem, photograph of Lincoln, King or Frederick Douglass on the classroom wall—the whole thing burns into the mind and stirs the life-desiring coals of pain and rage within the desperate consciousness of those who must repeatedly experience its bitterness.

If, to this sense of recent insult, insurrectionary anger, and sharp pain is added the exhilaration of the opening months and hours of a new and promising experience in the conception and then in the concrete, growing realization of the Free School, a fine, pure pitch of burning energy and of remarkable and unexpected confidence develops. It is the kind of time in which we grow and learn, and feel astonished at our capability to keep on going with so little rest or sleep. We live on doughnuts, glasses of milk, or hurried "potluck suppers" in the midst of wonderful, insane and crazy nights of money-raising tactics, strategies, campaigns, decide at midnight to put out a spectacular mailing the next morning, type up the stencils, ink over the millions of dumb errors that we make, dig up the minister friend of someone else's minister friend who said it was okay to use the ditto machine in someone else's Unitarian Church or someone's storefront office, break into the office, run off the stencils, do it ten times badly, finally get it almost right, breathe in the wonderful stink of the mimeograph ether, pile the new copies, staple, fold and label, find the misspelled headline just too late, argue and laugh, get out a bottle of cheap wine, drink from paper cups, go home and sleep four hours, wake up feeling terrific and then start all over.

"The exuberance of crisis," a group of my friends wrote when they were in the early stages of a kind of Free School venture of their own in Pennsylvania, "highlights the poverty of our daily experience.... The assertion of communal solidarity makes us feel more keenly the personal frustration of our normal routine. The expression of outrage against immediate evil bears the emotional intensity of all the anger unspoken each day, carries our entire burden of sadness and bitterness. The taste of revolution, the breath of promise it brings to our troubled lives, confirms the sense of desperation which we daily face."

Paulo Freire has written that one of the most familiar consequences of the "culture of silence," not only in the Third World but also in the internal colonies of the United States, is the loss of "subject status" in the consciousness of human beings, and in its place a sense of being always consequences ("objects") of the processes and the historical events initiated and conceived by others. If this is an accurate perception of our situation, then the kind of dynamic experience that I have just described is perhaps a classic example of the process of expropriation by the poor man of his own purloined and alienated sense of moral leverage. The saddening part, however, is the quite remarkable speed with which almost any process of creation and regeneration can become banal and routinized within this nation at the present time and, in this case, the quite astonishing speed with which a group of parents, children and their teachers can give up or somehow lose, even without the knowledge of the loss, that sense of passion and vocation that first burned within them.

The question, then, in my own sense of struggle, is as follows: How can the Free School achieve, at one and the same time, a sane, ongoing, down-to-earth, skill-oriented, sequential, credentializing and credentialized curricular experience directly geared-in to the real survival needs of colonized children in a competitive and technological society; and simultaneously evolve, maintain, nourish and revivify the "uncredentialized," "unauthorized," "unsanctioned," "noncurricular" consciousness of pain, rage, love, and revolution which first infused their little school with truth and magic, exhilaration and comradeship? Few schools up to now seem to have been able to do both; some that I know, however, come extremely close.

It is hard, I think, not to transform ourselves in six months or one year from a bold and eloquent brotherhood of strength, street logic, liberation, into a bunch of OEO-assisted, *New York Times*-admired, Model Cities-favored, Carnegie Foundation-visited "program administrators," "innovative educators," "resource people," "para-professionals" and all the rest. The very language used in the preceding phrases suggests the rapid degeneration of the Free School vision into a world of dull, unbrilliant, mediocre jargonese: "delivery of services," "secondary impact," "replicable features," "individualized curricula," "open-structured processes," "urban-oriented resource areas. . . ." If, on the one hand, the hang-loose hippie dialect represents a jargon of centrifugal release from sanity and honest and unarguable need, the bureaucratic jargonese reveals the still more devastating trap of Instantaneous Domestication. There has got to be a way to be "free" without being maniacally and insipidly euphoric, and to be consistent, strong, effective, but not tight-assed, businesslike and bureaucratic. Either direction represents a falling off from our original and authentic vision. The true, moral, political and semantic derivation of "Free School" lies in "Freedom School." It is to the liberation, to the vision and to the potency of the oppressed that any

Free School worth its derivation and its photographs of Neill, Tolstoi or Eldridge Cleaver must, in the long run, be accountable. If we lose this, in my judgment, we lose everything.

Several immediate tactical considerations seem to me to be a part of the above discussion: I think, first of all, that a great deal rests on physical location. The ideal location for a Free School born of the frustrations and the discontents of ten years' struggle to transform or liberate the public school is not across the city but *across the street* from that old, hated, but still-standing and still-murderous construction. I know that such an appropriate and explicit sense of physical confrontation is not always possible; nor, of course, does the visible reminder of the miserable and monolithic enemy assure the radical integrity or the revolutionary perseverance of the Free School on the opposite corner. It is, perhaps, a little easier and more sensible to state it in the opposite terms. A Free School which, by accident or intent, ends up in the most expensive, marginal and physically respectable section of a total neighborhood in torment is certainly a great deal more likely to lose sight of its own reason for existence than the school which, like the New School in its first three years in Boston, is straight across the street from that old haunted house that flies the U.S. flag, or which, like Harlem Prep, is in a renovated supermarket straight on Eighth Avenue in Harlem. The farther the distance from the place of pain, the less the reason to remember the oppressor's eyes or to be cognizant of his abiding powers.

It is hard, indeed, to worry about, or even really to believe in, the existence of lead-paint-poisoned infants or of vindictive, steel-eyed cops while strolling in the anesthetic gardens and the foliage-decorated courtyard of the Ford Foundation, still less in the privileged pavilions of somebody's all-white, upper-class Free School in the sloping mountains of Vermont or amid the red rocks and the perfect sunsets of Fort Collins, Colorado. The Free School that stands foursquare on the scene of struggle, in such physical, hard and graphic fashion as I have just proposed, cannot within the course of ordinary days fail to be stirred, provoked, inspired and at times enraged by concrete processes which take the form of real-life visions in the windowpane. Strong parents in the school across the street begin to organize. They want to know if we will let them use our school for their initial planning sessions. . . . Six of the younger and less domesticated teachers in the nearby junior high ask us if they could bring their kids into our "Black Action Workshop" after regular school hours. . . . They also ask us if we would support their presence at the School Committee Hearings on the following Wednesday night. . . . Two months later, three hundred kids and fourteen teachers from the same school stage a "walk-out." Their walk-out turns into a "walk-in," into the parent-operated Free School on the nearby corner. . . . Together we plan a picket line for Friday. . . . They hold "their" press conference in "our" kindergarten. . . . Our kindergarten kids unplug the

TV cables . . . interrupt the questions . . . humanize and give five minutes of excited, partisan and unexpected exhilaration to the press reporters who suddenly see, in the realization of our dream, what it is that those within the low-security prison on the opposite corner are protesting. . . .

This is the kind of high-stake and high-voltage substance and experience that make for permanent struggle and strong loyalties. In Roxbury, Massachusetts, on Leyland Street, a beautiful Free School, nourished and sustained by eloquent young parents and good teachers, discovers that several of its children are in grave medical danger as a consequence of lead poison in the nearby tenement houses. They canvass the neighborhood, enlist physicians, fire broadsides at the press. . . . Forty children in the neighborhood turn out to have been poisoned by the lead paint. . . . The school itself becomes the scene of medical examinations for all children, not just those who are the members of its student body. . . . The liberal press does one or two brief stories. . . . The courts do little . . . the city agencies still less. . . . In the winter, a child in Roxbury dies of lead-paint poison. . . .

The Free School is in the midst of true and human confrontation with the real world of exploitation and oppression that the law, the rental patterns and the medical profession constitute. Teachers at the school do not need to send away to Westinghouse or EDC for "relevant" social-studies units "oriented to some of the more serious issues in the urban situation." Most public schools, and a large number of the Free Schools too, nourish an atmosphere which is devoid of almost all true, credible experience and in which only arduous simulations of real processes take place. The ultimate paradox to which such gruesome institutions finally arrive is the introduction of that paradigm vehicle of school-delineated alienation—the "simulation game." We close up the windows, pull down the blinds, ventilate the air, deflect the light, absorb the sound, etherize the heart, and neutralize the soul; and then we bring in "simulation games" to try to imitate the world we have, with such great care and at such consummate expense, excluded. The twelve-million-dollar stone-and-concrete junior high school without walls and also without windows stands at the corner of the two most turbulent and most explosive streets within the "inner core." Inside, the "innovative," "open-structured" "teacher-as-a-resource-person" introduces to her locked-in class of black and militant, cheated and embittered eighth-grade children a "simulation game" called GHETTO: "Let's pretend now that we live within one of the racially impacted regions of the Northeast section of the country. . . ."

Alienation can seldom have reached a more exquisite pitch than this. The sadness, though, is that the Free School can with consummate ease develop the same ironical situation of the mirror created to reflect the real thing that we dare not look at. The reason, I suppose, that we fall into this state of mind so easily is just that so many of us, or almost all of us, have been "well schooled." As such, we think of school, even of Free School, in almost all of the same terms that we lived by when we were, ourselves, "schoolteachers" or "schoolchildren." The simulation ritual is the perfect metaphor of public education in its present form. The Free School that can break this mold of artifacted process receives the almost instantaneous reward not only in a heightened sense of loyalty and strength in its adult ranks but also in the sense of strong and unmanipulated motivation on the part of its own children. It doesn't take a lot of bullshit speeches about the need of a neighborhood for good black doctors, lab technicians, chemists, biologists, biochemical analysts and such, when the little boy across the street dies of the lead paint on the walls of his own bedroom.

"Relevance" and "urban-oriented" are the twin curricular code phrases in this nation, at the present time, for the ritual experience of looking into the mirror at the battle being waged behind our back while walking rapidly away from it. The Free School that shatters the mirror and turns to face the flames is the one that will not lose its consciousness of struggle or its capability for a continual process of regeneration. When we forget the enemy's name, we turn our guns upon each other. The guerrilla martyrs who lost their lives within the mountains of Bolivia understood this very, very well. Morale declined, paranoia thrived, internal decimation soared, when the periods of time between significant confrontations grew too many and too long extended. Free School parents in Boston and New York begin to turn their guns on one another, and on their chosen teachers and their own Headmaster and Headmistress too, only when they forget the power and calculation of a man like Albert Shanker or the personal brutalism of a woman like Louise Day Hicks. The location of the Free School, the vivid and repeated confrontations in which it is willing to engage with the immediate manifestations of municipal exploitation on all sides, the degree to which it identifies its own survival with the struggle of those across the street who still are locked within the public prisons—these are the kinds of things which seem to me a great deal more important than the number of stamped and sanctioned "innovative methods" that we bring into our little space of liberation, learning and regeneration.

In his book *The Storefront,* Ned O'Gorman writes these words:

> A fire inspector comes to bug us about a minor violation. . . . I take him out onto the sidewalk and shout out loud to the people there, and to the people looking out of windows that finally someone has come to inspect their houses and do something about their suffering. . . . The inspector knows and I know that he has come to bug the storefront. . . . In the guise of inspectors the city suddenly appears to check up on restaurants,

schools, shops, day-care centers, and playgrounds. Yet families can suffer an entire winter without heat or hot water and no inspector ever appears to challenge the landlord.

This passage, brief and offhand as it seems, says a great deal of what I have been trying to express about the sense of consciousness, of permanent struggle, and of immediate, unmanipulated, honest activism within the context of a Free School. There is much within O'Gorman's book that I do not agree with; in this regard, however, I am in complete accord with his whole impulse and with his instinctive way of getting mad. It seems to me of great importance that we do not forget how to get very, very mad, and at which people.

Jonathan Kozol asked us to print the following pitch for the Education Action Fund:

There is one other method of fund-raising which I did not mention in the earlier pages of this book. This is the method of writing a little book to share some of the struggles and some of the challenges and some of the details that a Free School needs to deal with. This is, of course, one of the motives for the publication of this handbook. My wife and I intend to share the proceeds from its sale with several of the Free Schools that we know firsthand, admire and believe in. Those who would like to add their own small offerings to ours are invited to send nonprofit contributions to the Education Action Fund, Inc., P.O. Box 27, Essex Station, Boston, Massachusetts 02112, a tax-exempt trust which will distribute funds to a number of Free Schools serving black, poor white or Spanish-speaking neighborhoods in several cities.

DESCHOOLING

The two essays which follow, by Paul Goodman and Ivan Illich, represent the furthest edges of pedagogic thought, the point at which a belief in schools (even free schools) is replaced by a search for alternatives to them. The schools are seen as part of a larger problem, what one might call the increasing institutionalization of private experience, and schooling itself is seen as the expression and reification of that process. Both Goodman and Illich see in the schools the means by which the possibilities of independent and associative activity are constrained or destroyed, and both of them put more faith in the unmanaged cooperation of men and women than in the centralized institutions which replace them. Illich's two books, *Deschooling Society* and *Tools for Conviviality*, are attempts to establish imaginative alternatives to the systems now at work and spreading, and almost all of Goodman's work, including his fiction, offers in one form or another libertarian solutions to the same problems. He is an anarchist, a communitarian, and one of his books, *Communitas*, spells out in detail his suggestions for more sensible ways to organize society economically and politically.

Both Goodman and Illich understand, then, that "deschooling" is something that depends upon the de-institutionalization of other aspects of the society, and that the schools can only be replaced, ultimately, by the kinds of community which sustain relations between elders and the young and which are, by their very nature, educative through participation, through free activity. None of that, of course, means an end to learning or an end to knowledge; it simply means making them a function of social relations rather than the state, of community rather than institutions. But that, as Goodman and Illich know, will not happen until larger changes have occurred, changes in the ways we view human nature and possibility, changes in the way we think about institutions and the state. It is, at bottom, those larger changes which interest them, and talking about schools is simply one of the easiest ways to get at them.

And yet, in another way, deschooling is neither a grand nor a frightening idea. Most of us, when we think of it, envision the children let loose from the schools and running wild in the streets, like something out of *Lord of the Flies*. We picture them as savages, unable to read or think, deprived of the wisdom of the culture. But that is not at all what Illich or Goodman are after; indeed, what interests them is the restoration of the knowledge and culture which they believe are destroyed in schools. What they want in the way of education is simply an extension of the ways we are together, privately, most of the time. One can think of several examples of cooperative activity: consumer co-ops, town meetings, communes, college fraternities and sororities, clubs, encounter groups, even adolescent gangs and children's games. In all of those activities people agree to various limits and common aims and abide by them without coercion, and in all of them they learn on their own whatever they feel is necessary to their own ends and needs. In that sense, at least, "deschooling" does not mean an end to participation in society or respect for culture. It means, simply, a willingness to let the human impulse toward those things express itself more fully and sensibly, on a more human scale, and in a more organic way. It is intended to be a liberation of both intelligence and energy, and it is founded, of course, on the belief that people are capable of the same kinds of concern and devotion that their leaders and bureaucrats are.

One of the easiest ways to deschool ourselves, for instance, would simply be to eliminate the compulsory education laws at the same time that we put into effect the voucher system and "professionalize" teachers so that they could practice in much the same way that doctors, lawyers and counselors do. In all those professions, once licensed by the state, one is free to practice as one wishes: independently, in partnership, in a small group (a clinic or firm), or for a larger institution like a hospital. The independent practitioner is equivalent to the tutor; the group is like a free school; the hospital is like the public school. It would be possible for teachers to practice in the same way, with all those options, but they do not have those choices. They are still trained, pushed and allowed to work only for the public schools or other large and privately financed schools (usually as institutional in nature as the state's, like Catholic schools). Teachers cannot hang out a shingle and practice independently. Nursery-school teachers can, as can baby-sitters, and tennis coaches, and voice experts, and dog trainers, and art instructors. Though teachers of reading, writing, mathematics and so on might be treated in the same way, they are not; those subjects are monopolized by the state, and through that monopoly it maintains its hold on the children themselves—and, through them, on all thought, all imagination. Were we willing to give that up, the state might content itself with licensing teachers on the basis of a minimal competence determined by examination. Teachers themselves, like lawyers, doctors and psychologists, could maintain on their own certain guildlike standards of competence. Children, in turn, might be expected to achieve minimal standards of literacy and/or skillfulness, and they would be free to achieve that in any way they could: by attending a large public school, visiting a store-front tutor a few hours a week, learning on their own, etc. If coupled with the voucher plan this would set both the young and their elders free to form a new set of relations based on need, will and affection, and the state would simply make available (through the return of tax monies or tax deductions) the money necessary for parents to pay their children's schools and teachers.

There is nothing very apocalyptic about such a plan, and it is only a minimal kind of deschooling, but we are not likely to do anything like that for decades, if ever we do. Such a system would mean not only suppressing our strong urge to contain and control the free play of energies, it would mean a willingness to entirely remake our communities in ways that would provide for the young a whole range of activities now missing. Our communities, now organized consciously around the existence of schools, would have to be rethought, reinvented, to accommodate this kind of change. But the fact is that we seem to feel collectively that we cannot make such changes, and that we must therefore keep the young in the schools. That means they too, in turn, will think institutionally as adults, will not imagine large changes possible, and it is in that way that the wheel goes round and round, institutionalization increasing all the time.

The suggestions Goodman and Illich make seem utopian only because of the ways we think—not because they cannot be put to use. They are "idealistic" merely because most of us seem caught forever among the small changes that never quite work and which make in the end no difference at all. Goodman and Illich are speaking about *practical* things, about the only solutions which may help us get out of the trap we are in; but how many people will see that?

PAUL GOODMAN
The Universal Trap

A conference of experts on school drop-outs will discuss the background of poverty, cultural deprivation, race prejudice, family and emotional troubles, neighborhood uprooting, urban mobility. It will explore ingenious expedients to counteract these conditions, though it will not much look to remedying them—that is not its business. And it will suggest propaganda—e.g., no school, no job—to get the youngsters back in school. It is axiomatic that they ought to be in school.

After a year, it proves necessary to call another conference to cope with the alarming fact that more than 75% of the drop-outs who have been cajoled into returning, having dropped out again. They persist in failing; they are not sufficiently motivated. What curricular changes must there be? How can the teachers learn the life-style of the underprivileged?

Curiously muffled in these conferences is the question that puts the burden of proof the other way: What are they drop-outs from? Is the schooling really good for them, or much good for anybody? Since, for many, there are such difficulties with the present arrangements, might not some better arrangements be invented? Or bluntly, since schooling undertakes to be compulsory, must it not continually review its claim to be useful? Is it the only means of education? Isn't it unlikely that *any* single type of social institution could fit almost every youngster up to age 16 and beyond? (It is predicted that by 1970, 50% will go to college.)

But conferences on drop-outs are summoned by school professionals, so perhaps we cannot hope that such elementary questions will be raised. Yet neither are they raised by laymen. There is a mass superstition, underwritten by additional billions every year, that adolescents must continue

"The Universal Trap" is reprinted by permission of the publisher, Horizon Press, from *Compulsory Mis-Education* by Paul Goodman. Copyright © 1964.

going to school. The middle-class *know* that no professional competence —i.e., status and salary—can be attained without many diplomas; and poor people have allowed themselves to be convinced that the primary remedy for their increasing deprivation is to agitate for better schooling. Nevertheless, I doubt that, *at present or with any reforms that are conceivable under present school administration,* going to school is the best use for the time of life of the majority of youth.

Education is a natural community function and occurs inevitably, since the young grow up on the old, toward their activities, and into (or against) their institutions; and the old foster, teach, train, exploit, and abuse the young. Even neglect of the young, except physical neglect, has an educational effect—not the worst possible.

Formal schooling is a reasonable auxiliary of the inevitable process, whenever an activity is best learned by singling it out for special attention with a special person to teach it. Yet it by no means follows that the complicated artifact of a school system has much to do with education, and certainly not with good education.

Let us bear in mind the way in which a big school system might have nothing to do with education at all. The New York system turns over $700 millions annually, not including capital improvements. There are 750 schools, with perhaps 15 annually being replaced at an extra cost of $2 to $5 millions each. There are 40,000 paid employees. This is a vast vested interest, and it is very probable that—like much of our economy and almost all of our political structure, of which the public schools are a part—it goes on for its own sake, keeping more than a million people busy, wasting wealth, and preempting time and space in which something else could be going on. It is a gigantic market for textbook manufacturers, building contractors, and graduate-schools of Education.

The fundamental design of such a system is ancient, yet it has not been altered although the present operation is altogether different in scale from what it was, and therefore it must have a different meaning. For example, in 1900, 6% of the 17-year-olds graduated from high school, and less than ½% went to college; whereas in 1963, 65% graduated from high school and 35% went on to something called college. Likewise, there is a vast difference between schooling intermitted in life on a farm or in a city with plenty of small jobs, and schooling that is a child's only "serious" occupation and often his only adult contact. Thus, a perhaps outmoded institution has become almost the only allowable way of growing up. And with this pre-empting, there is an increasing intensification of the one narrow experience, e.g., in the shaping of the curriculum and testing according to the increasing requirements of graduate schools far off in time and place. Just as our American society as a whole is more and more tightly organized, so its school system is more and more regimented as part of that organization.

The Universal Trap 61

In the organizational plan the schools play a non-educational and an educational role. The non-educational role is very important. In the tender grades, the schools are a baby-sitting service during a period of collapse of the old-type family and during a time of extreme urbanization and urban mobility. In the junior and senior high school grades, they are an arm of the police, providing cops and concentration camps paid for in the budget under the heading "Board of Education." The educational role is, by and large, to provide—at public and parents' expense—apprentice-training for corporations, government, and the teaching profession itself, and also to train the young, as New York's Commissioner of Education has said (in the Worley case), "to handle constructively their problems of adjustment to authority."

The public schools of America have indeed been a powerful, and beneficent, force for the democratizing of a great mixed population. But we must be careful to keep reassessing them when, with changing conditions, they become a universal trap and democracy begins to look like regimentation.

Let me spend a page on the history of the compulsory nature of the school systems. In 1961, in *The Child, the Parent, and the State,* James Conant mentions a possible incompatibility between "individual development" and "national needs"; this, to my mind, is a watershed in American philosophy of education and puts us back to the ideology of Imperial Germany, or on a par with contemporary Russia.

When Jefferson and Madison conceived of compulsory schooling, such an incompatibility would have been unthinkable. They were in the climate of the Enlightenment, were strongly influenced by Congregational (town-meeting) ideas, and were of course makers of a revolution. To them, "citizen" meant society-*maker,* not one "participating in" or "adjusted to" society. It is clear that they regarded themselves and their friends as citizens existentially, so to speak; to make society was their breath of life. But obviously such conceptions are worlds removed from, and diametrically opposed to, our present political reality, where the ground rules and often the score are pre-determined.

For Jefferson, people had to be taught in order to multiply the sources of citizenly initiative and to be vigilant for freedom. Everybody had to become literate and study history, in order to make constitutional innovations and be fired to defend free institutions, which was presumably the moral that history taught. And those of good parts were to study a technological natural philosophy, in order to make inventions and produce useful goods for the new country. By contrast, what are the citizenly reasons for which we compel everybody to be literate, etc.? To keep the economy expanding, to understand the mass-communications, to choose between indistinguishable Democrats and Republicans. Planning and decision-making are lodged in top managers; rarely, and at most, the electorate serves as a pressure-group. There is a new emphasis on teaching science but the vast majority will never use this knowledge and will forget it; they are consumers.

Another great impulse for compulsory education came from the new industrialism and urbanism during the three or four decades after the Civil War, a time also of maximum immigration. Here the curricular demands were more mundane: in the grades, literacy and arithmetic; in the colleges, professional skills to man the expanding economy. But again, no one would have spoken of an incompatibility between "individual development" and "national needs," for it was considered to be an open society, abounding in opportunity. Topically, the novels of Horatio Alger, Jr., treat schooling as morally excellent as well as essential for getting ahead; and there is no doubt that the immigrants saw education-for-success as also a human value for their children. Further, the school-system was not a trap. The 94% who in 1900 did not finish high school had other life opportunities, including making a lot of money and rising in politics. But again, by and large this is not our present situation. There is plenty of social mobility, opportunity to rise—except precisely for the ethnic minorities who are our main concern as drop-outs—but the statuses and channels are increasingly stratified, rigidified, cut and dried. Most enterprise is parceled out by feudal corporations, or by the state; and these determine the requirements. Ambition with average talent meets these rules or fails; those without relevant talent, or with unfortunate backgrounds, cannot even survive in decent poverty. The requirements of survival are importantly academic, attainable only in schools and universities; but such schooling is ceasing to have an initiating or moral meaning.

We do not have an open economy; even when jobs are not scarce, the corporations and state dictate the possibilities of enterprise. General Electric swoops down on the high schools, or IBM on the colleges, and skims off the youth who have been pre-trained for them at public or private expense. (Private college tuition runs upward of $6000, and this is estimated as a third or less of the actual cost for "education and educational administration.") Even a department store requires a diploma for its salespeople, not so much because of the skills they have learned as that it guarantees the right character: punctual and with a smooth record. And more generally, since our powers-that-be have opted for an expanding economy with a galloping standard of living, and since the powers of the world are in an arms and space race, there *is* a national need for many graduates specifically trained. Thus, even for those selected, the purpose is irrelevant to citizenly initiative, the progress of an open society, or personal happiness, and the others have spent time and effort in order to be progressively weeded out. Some drop out.

It is said that our schools are geared to "middle-class values," but this is a false and misleading use of terms. The schools less and less represent *any* human values, but simply adjustment to a mechanical system.

Because of the increasing failure of the schools with the poor urban mass, there has developed a line of criticism—e.g., Oscar Lewis, Patricia Sexton, Frank Riessman, and even Edgar Friedenberg—asserting that there is a "culture of poverty" which the "middle-class" schools do not fit, but which has its own virtues of spontaneity, sociality, animality. The implication is that the "middle class," for all its virtues, is obsessional, prejudiced, prudish.

Pedagogically, this insight is indispensable. A teacher must try to reach each child in terms of what he brings, his background, his habits, the language he understands. But if taken to be more than technical, it is a disastrous conception. The philosophic aim of education must be to get each one out of his isolated class and into the one humanity. Prudence and responsibility are not middle-class virtues but human virtues; and spontaneity and sexuality are not powers of the simple but of human health. One has the impression that our social-psychologists are looking not to a human community but to a future in which the obsessionals will take care of the impulsives!

In fact, some of the most important strengths that have historically belonged to the middle class are flouted by the schools: independence, initiative, scrupulous honesty, earnestness, utility, respect for thorough scholarship. Rather than bourgeois, our schools have become pettybourgeois, bureaucratic, time-serving, gradegrind-practical, timid, and *nouveau riche* climbing. In the upper grades and colleges, they often exude a cynicism that belongs to rotten aristocrats.

Naturally, however, the youth of the poor and of the middle class respond differently to the petty-bourgeois atmosphere. For many poor children, school is orderly and has food, compared to chaotic and hungry homes, and it might even be interesting compared to total deprivation of toys and books. Besides, the wish to improve a child's lot, which on the part of a middle class parent might be frantic status-seeking and pressuring, on the part of a poor parent is a loving aspiration. There is here a gloomy irony. The school that for a poor Negro child might be a great joy and opportunity is likely to be dreadful; whereas the middle class child might be better off *not* in the "good" suburban school he has.

Other poor youth, herded into a situation that does not fit their disposition, for which they are unprepared by their background, and which does not interest them, simply develop a reactive stupidity very different from their behavior on the street or ball field. They fall behind, play truant, and as soon as possible drop out. If the school situation is immediately useless and damaging to them, their response must be said to be life-preservative.

The reasonable social policy would be not to have these youth in school, certainly not in high school, but to educate them otherwise and provide opportunity for a decent future in some other way. How? In my opinion, the wise thing would be to have our conferences on *this* issue, and omit the idea of drop-out altogether. But the brute fact is that our society isn't really interested; the concern for the drop-outs is mainly because they are a nuisance and a threat and can't be socialized by the existing machinery.

Numerically far more important than these overt drop-outs at 16, however, are the children who conform to schooling between the ages of 6 to 16 or 20, but who drop out internally and day-dream, their days wasted, their liberty caged and scheduled. And there are many such in the middle class, from backgrounds with plenty of food and some books and art, where the youth is seduced by the prospect of money and status but even more where he is terrified to jeopardize the only pattern of life he knows.

It is in the schools and from the mass media, rather than at home or from their friends, that the mass of our citizens in all classes learn that life is inevitably routine, depersonalized, venally graded; that it is best to toe the mark and shut up; that there is no place for spontaneity, open sexuality, free spirit. Trained in the schools, they go on to the same quality of jobs, culture, politics. This *is* education, mis-education, socializing to the national norms and regimenting to the national "needs."

John Dewey used to hope, naively, that the schools could be a community somewhat better than society and serve as a lever for social change. In fact, our schools reflect our society closely, except that they *emphasize* many of its worst features, as well as having the characteristic defects of academic institutions of all times and places.

Can it be denied that in some respects the drop-outs make a wiser choice than many who go to school, not to get real goods but to get money? Their choice of the "immediate"—their notorious "inability to tolerate delay"—is not altogether impulsive and neurotic. The bother is that in our present culture, which puts its entire emphasis on the consumption of expensive commodities, they are so nagged by inferiority, exclusion, and despair of the future that they cannot enjoy their leisure with a good conscience. Because they know little, they are deprived of many profound simple satisfactions and they never know what to do with themselves. Being afraid of exposing themselves to awkwardness and ridicule, they just hang around. And our urban social arrangements— e.g., high rent—have made it impossible for anybody to be decently poor on a "low" standard. One is either in the rat-race or has dropped out of society altogether.

As a loyal academic, I must make a further observation. Mainly to provide Ph.D.'s, there is at present an overwhelming pressure to gear the "better" elementary schools to the graduate-universities. This is the great current reform, genre of Rickover. But what if the top of the ladder is corrupt and corrupts the lower grades? On visits to 70 colleges everywhere in the country, I have been appalled at how rarely the subjects are studied in a right academic spirit, for their truth and beauty and as part of humane international culture. The students are given, and seek, a narrow expertise, "mastery," aimed at licenses and salary. They are indoctrinated with a national thoughtlessness that is not even chauvinistic. Administrators sacrifice the community of scholars to aggrandizement and extramurally sponsored research.

Conversely, there is almost never conveyed the sense in which learning is truly practical, to enlighten experience, give courage to initiate and change, reform the state, deepen personal and social peace. On the contrary, the entire educational system itself creates professional cynicism or the resigned conviction that Nothing Can Be Done. If this is the University, how can we hope for aspiring scholarship in the elementary schools? On the contrary, everything will be grades and conforming, getting ahead not in the subject of interest but up the ladder. Students "do" Bronx Science in order to "make" M.I.T. and they "do" M.I.T. in order to "make" Westinghouse; some of them have "done" Westinghouse in order to "make" jail.

What then? The compulsory system has become a universal trap, and it is no good. Very many of the youth, both poor and middle class, might be better off if the system simply did not exist, even if they then had no formal schooling at all. (I am extremely curious for a philosophic study of Prince Edward County in Virginia, where for some years schooling did not exist for Negro children.)

But what would become of these children? For very many, both poor and middle class, their homes are worse than the schools, and the city streets are worse in another way. Our urban and suburban environments are precisely not cities or communities where adults naturally attend to the young and educate to a viable life. Also, perhaps especially in the case of the overt drop-outs, the state of their body and soul is such that we must give them refuge and remedy, whether it be called school, settlement house, youth worker, or work camp.

There are thinkable alternatives. Here are half a dozen directly relevant to the subject we have been discussing, the system as compulsory trap. In principle, when a law begins to do more harm than good, the best policy is to alleviate it or try doing without it.

i. Have "no school at all" for a few classes. These children should be selected from tolerable, though not necessarily cultured, homes. They should be neighbors and numerous enough to be a society for one another and so that they do not feel merely "different." Will they learn the rudiments anyway? This experiment cannot do the children any academic harm, since there is good evidence that normal children will make up the first seven years school-work with four to seven months of good teaching.

ii. Dispense with the school building for a few classes; provide teachers and use the city itself as the school—its streets, cafeterias, stores, movies, museums, parks, and factories. Where feasible, it certainly makes more sense to teach using the real subject-matter than to bring an abstraction of the subject-matter into the schoolbuilding as "curriculum." Such a class should probably not exceed 10 children for one pedagogue. The idea—it is the model of Athenian education—is not dissimilar to youth gang work, but not applied to delinquents and not playing to the gang ideology.

iii. Along the same lines, but both outside and inside the school building, use appropriate *unlicensed* adults of the community—the druggist, the storekeeper, the mechanic—as the proper educators of the young into the grown-up world. By this means we can try to overcome the separation of the young from the grown-up world so characteristic in modern urban life, and to diminish the omnivorous authority of the professional school-people. Certainly it would be a useful and animating experience for the adults. (There is the beginning of such a volunteer program in the New York and some other systems.)

iv. Make class attendance not compulsory, in the manner of A. S. Neill's Summerhill. If the teachers are good, absence would tend to be eliminated; if they are bad, let them know it. The compulsory law is useful to get the children away from the parents, but it must not result in trapping the children. A fine modification of this suggestion is the rule used by Frank Brown in Florida: he permits the children to be absent for a week or a month to engage in any worthwhile enterprise or visit any new environment.

v. Decentralize an urban school (or do not build a new big building) into small units, 20 to 50, in available store-fronts or clubhouses. These tiny schools equipped with record-player and pin-ball machine, could combine play, socializing, discussion, and formal teaching. For special events, the small units can be brought together into a common auditorium or gymnasium, so as to give the sense of the greater community. Correspondingly, I think it would be worthwhile to give the Little Red Schoolhouse a spin under modern urban conditions, and see how it works out: that is, to combine all the ages in a little room for 25 to 30, rather than to grade by age.

vi. Use a pro rata part of the school money to send children to economically marginal farms for a couple of months of the year, perhaps 6 children from mixed backgrounds to a farmer. The only requirement is that the farmer feed them and not beat them; best, of course, if they take part in the farm-work. This will give the farmer cash, as part of the generally desirable program to redress the urban-rural ratio to something nearer to 70% to 30%. (At present, less than 8% of families are rural.) Conceivably, some of the urban children will take to the other way of life, and we might generate a new kind of rural culture.

I frequently suggest these and similar proposals at teachers colleges, and I am looked at with an eerie look—do I really mean to *diminish* the state-aid grant for each student-day? But mostly the objection is that such proposals entail intolerable administrative difficulties.

Above all; we must apply these or any other proposals to particular individuals and small groups, without the obligation of uniformity. There is a case for uniform standards of achievement, lodged in the Regents, but they *cannot* be reached by uniform techniques. The claim that standardization of procedure is more efficient, less costly, or alone administratively practical, is often false. Particular inventiveness requires thought, but thought does not cost money.

IVAN ILLICH
The Alternative to Schooling

For several years at CIDOC in Cuernavaca we have conducted critical research on the monopoly of the industrial mode of production and have tried to define conceptually alternative modes that would fit a postindustrial age. During the late sixties this research centered on educational devices. By 1970 we had found that:

1. Universal education through compulsory schooling is not possible.

2. Alternative devices for the production and marketing of mass education are technically more feasible and ethically less tolerable than compulsory graded schools. Such new educational arrangements are now on the verge of replacing traditional school systems in rich and in poor countries. They are potentially more effective in the conditioning of job-holders and consumers in an industrial economy. They are therefore more attractive for the management of present societies, more seductive for the people, and insidiously destructive of fundamental values.

3. A society committed to high levels of shared learning and critical personal intercourse must set pedagogical limits on industrial growth.

I have published the results of this research in a previous volume of World Perspectives, *entitled* Deschooling Society. *I clarified some of the points left ill defined in that book by writing an article published in the* Saturday Review *of April 19, 1971.*

Our analysis of schooling has led us to recognize the mass production of education as a paradigm for other industrial enterprises, each producing a service commodity, each organized as a public utility, and each defining its output as a basic necessity. At first our attention was drawn

"The Alternative to Schooling" by Ivan Illich, from the *Saturday Review* of April 19, 1971. Used by permission of Ivan Illich. The introduction to this article is abridged from the Introduction to *Tools of Conviviality,* copyright © 1973 by Ivan Illich, used by permission of Harper & Row, Publishers.

69

to *the compulsory insurance of professional health care, and to systems of public transport, which tend to become compulsory once traffic rolls above a certain speed. We found that the industrialization of any service agency leads to destructive side effects analogous to the unwanted secondary results well known from the overproduction of goods. We had to face a set of limits to growth in the service sector of any society as inescapable as the limits inherent in the industrial production of artifacts. We concluded that a set of limits to industrial growth is well formulated only if these limits apply both to goods and to services which are produced in an industrial mode. So we set out to clarify these limits.*

I here submit the concept of a multidimensional balance of human life which can serve as a framework for evaluating man's relation to his tools. In each of several dimensions of this balance it is possible to identify a natural scale. When an enterprise grows beyond a certain point on this scale, it first frustrates the end for which it was originally designed, and then rapidly becomes a threat to society itself. These scales must be identified and the parameters of human endeavors within which human life remains viable must be explored. . . .

For generations we have tried to make the world a better place by providing more and more schooling, but so far the endeavor has failed. What we have learned instead is that forcing all children to climb an open-ended education ladder cannot enhance equality but must favor the individual who starts out earlier, healthier, or better prepared; that enforced instruction deadens for most people the will for independent learning; and that knowledge treated as a commodity, delivered in packages, and accepted as private property once it is acquired, must always be scarce.

In response, critics of the educational system are now proposing strong and unorthodox remedies that range from the voucher plan, which would enable each person to buy the education of his choice on an open market, to shifting the responsibility for education from the school to the media and to apprenticeship on the job. Some individuals foresee that the school will have to be disestablished just as the church was disestablished all over the world during the last two centuries. Other reformers propose to replace the universal school with various new systems that would, they claim, better prepare everybody for life in modern society. These proposals for new educational institutions fall into three broad categories: the reformation of the classroom within the school system; the dispersal of free schools throughout society; and the transformation of all society into one huge classroom. But these three approaches—the reformed classroom, the free school, and the worldwide classroom—represent three stages in a proposed escalation of education in which each step threatens more subtle and more pervasive social control than the one it replaces.

I believe that the disestablishment of the school has become inevitable and that this end of an illusion should fill us with hope. But I also believe that the end of the "age of schooling" could usher in the epoch of the global schoolhouse that would be distinguishable only in name from a global madhouse or global prison in which education, correction, and adjustment become synonymous. I therefore believe that the breakdown of the school forces us to look beyond its imminent demise and to face fundamental alternatives in education. Either we can work for fearsome and potent new educational devices that teach about a world which progressively becomes more opaque and forbidding for man, or we can set the conditions for a new era in which technology would be used to make society more simple and transparent, so that all men can once again know the facts and use the tools that shape their lives. In short, we can disestablish schools or we can deschool culture.

In order to see clearly the alternatives we face, we must first distinguish education from schooling, which means separating the humanistic intent of the teacher from the impact of the invariant structure of the school. This hidden structure constitutes a course of instruction that stays forever beyond the control of the teacher or of his school board. It conveys indelibly the message that only through schooling can an individual prepare himself for adulthood in society, that what is not taught in school is of little value, and that what is learned outside of school is not worth knowing. I call it the hidden curriculum of schooling, because it constitutes the unalterable framework of the system, within which all changes in the curriculum are made.

The hidden curriculum is always the same regardless of school or place. It requires all children of a certain age to assemble in groups of about thirty, under the authority of a certified teacher, for some 500 to 1,000 or more hours each year. It doesn't matter whether the curriculum is designed to teach the principles of fascism, liberalism, Catholicism, or socialism; or whether the purpose of the school is to produce Soviet or United States citizens, mechanics, or doctors. It makes no difference whether the teacher is authoritarian or permissive, whether he imposes his own creed or teaches students to think for themselves. What is important is that students learn that education is valuable when it is acquired in the school through a graded process of consumption; that the degree of success the individual will enjoy in society depends on the amount of learning he consumes; and that learning *about* the world is more valuable than learning *from* the world.

It must be clearly understood that the hidden curriculum translates learning from an activity into a commodity—for which the school monopolizes the market. In all countries knowledge is regarded as the first necessity for survival, but also as a form of currency more liquid than rubles or dollars. We have become accustomed, through Karl Marx's writings, to speak about the alienation of the worker from his work in a class society. We must now recognize the estrangement of man from his learning when it becomes the product of a service profession and he becomes the consumer.

The more learning an individual consumes, the more "knowledge stock" he acquires. The hidden curriculum therefore defines a new class structure for society within which the large consumers of knowledge—those who have acquired large quantities of knowledge stock—enjoy special privileges, high income, and access to the more powerful tools of production. This kind of knowledge-capitalism has been accepted in all industrialized societies and establishes a rationale for the distribution of jobs and income. (This point is especially important in the light of the lack of correspondence between schooling and occupational competence established in studies such as Ivar Berg's *Education and Jobs: The Great Training Robbery*.)

The endeavor to put all men through successive stages of enlightenment is rooted deeply in alchemy, the Great Art of the waning Middle Ages. John Amos Comenius, a Moravian bishop, self-styled Pansophist, and pedagogue, is rightly considered one of the founders of the modern schools. He was among the first to propose seven or twelve grades of compulsory learning. In his *Magna Didactica*, he described schools as devices to "teach everybody everything" and outlined a blueprint for the assembly-line production of knowledge, which according to his method would make education cheaper and better and make growth into full humanity possible for all. But Comenius was not only an early efficiency expert, he was an alchemist who adopted the technical language of his craft to describe the art of rearing children. The alchemist sought to refine base elements by leading their distilled spirits through twelve stages of successive enlightenment, so that for their own and all the world's benefit they might be transmuted into gold. Of course, alchemists failed no matter how often they tried, but each time their "science" yielded new reasons for their failure, and they tried again.

Pedagogy opened a new chapter in the history of Ars Magna. Education became the search for an alchemic process that would bring forth a new type of man, who would fit into an environment created by scientific magic. But, no matter how much each generation spent on its schools, it always turned out that the majority of people were unfit for enlightenment by this process and had to be discarded as unprepared for life in a man-made world.

Educational reformers who accept the idea that schools have failed fall into three groups. The most respectable are certainly the great masters of alchemy who promise better schools. The most seductive are popular magicians, who promise to make every kitchen into an alchemic lab. The most sinister are the new Masons of the Universe, who want to transform the entire world into one huge temple of learning. Notable among today's masters of alchemy are certain research directors employed or sponsored by the large foundations who believe that schools, if they could somehow be improved, could also become economically more feasible than those that are now in trouble, and simultaneously could sell a larger package of services. Those who are concerned primarily with the curriculum claim that it is outdated or irrelevant. So the curriculum is filled with new packaged courses on African Culture, North American Imperialism, Women's Lib, Pollution, or the Consumer Society. Passive learning is wrong—it is indeed—so we graciously allow students to decide what and how they want to be taught. Schools are prison houses. Therefore, principals are authorized to approve teach-outs, moving the school desks to a roped-off Harlem street. Sensitivity training becomes fashionable. So, we import group therapy into the classroom. School, which was supposed to teach everybody everything, now becomes all things to all children.

Other critics emphasize that schools make inefficient use of modern science. Some would administer drugs to make it easier for the instructor to change the child's behavior. Others would transform school into a stadium for educational gaming. Still others would electrify the classroom. If they are simplistic disciples of McLuhan, they replace blackboards and textbooks with multimedia happenings; if they follow Skinner, they claim to be able to modify behavior more efficiently than old-fashioned classroom practitioners can.

Most of these changes have, of course, some good effects. The experimental schools have fewer truants. Parents do have a greater feeling of participation in a decentralized district. Pupils, assigned by their teacher to an apprenticeship, do often turn out more competent than those who stay in the classroom. Some children do improve their knowledge of Spanish in the language lab because they prefer playing with the knobs of a tape recorder to conversations with their Puerto Rican peers. Yet all these improvements operate within predictably narrow limits, since they leave the hidden curriculum of school intact.

Some reformers would like to shake loose from the hidden curriculum, but they rarely succeed. Free schools that lead to further free schools produce a mirage of freedom, even though the chain of attendance is frequently interrupted by long stretches of loafing. Attendance through seduction inculcates the need for educational treatment more persuasively than the reluctant attendance enforced by a truant officer. Permissive teachers in a padded classroom can easily render their pupils impotent to survive once they leave.

Learning in these schools often remains nothing more than the acquisition of socially valued skills defined, in this instance, by the consensus of a commune rather than by the decree of a school board. New presbyter is but old priest writ large.

Free schools, to be truly free, must meet two conditions: First, they must be run in a way to prevent the reintroduction of the hidden curriculum of graded attendance and certified students studying at the feet of certified teachers. And, more importantly, they must provide a framework in which all participants—staff and pupils—can free themselves from the hidden foundations of a schooled society. The first condition is frequently incorporated in the stated aims of a free school. The second condition is only rarely recognized, and is difficult to state as the goal of a free school.

It is useful to distinguish between the hidden curriculum, which I have described, and the occult foundations of schooling. The hidden curriculum is a ritual that can be considered the official initiation into modern society, institutionally established through the school. It is the purpose of this ritual to hide from its participants the contradictions between the myth of an egalitarian society and the class-conscious reality it certifies. Once they are recognized as such, rituals lose their power, and this is what is now beginning to happen to schooling. But there are certain fundamental assumptions about growing up—the occult foundations—which now find their expression in the ceremonial of schooling, and which could easily be reinforced by what free schools do.

Among these assumptions is what Peter Schrag calls the "immigration syndrome," which impels us to treat all people as if they were newcomers who must go through a naturalization process. Only certified consumers of knowledge are admitted to citizenship. Men are not born equal, but are made equal through gestation by Alma Mater.

The rhetoric of all schools states that they form a man for the future, but they do not release him for his task before he has developed a high level of tolerance to the ways of his elders: education *for* life rather than *in* everyday life. Few free schools can avoid doing precisely this. Nevertheless they are among the most important centers from which a new life-style radiates, not because of the effect their graduates will have but, rather, because elders who choose to bring up their children without the benefit of properly ordained teachers frequently belong to a radical minority and because their preoccupation with the rearing of their children sustains them in their new style.

The most dangerous category of educational reformer is one who argues that knowledge can be produced and sold much more effectively on an open market than on one controlled by school. These people argue that most skills can be easily acquired from skill-models if the learner is truly interested in their acquisition; that individual entitlements can provide a more equal purchasing power for education. They demand a careful separation of the process by which knowledge is acquired from the process by which it is measured and certified. These seem to me obvious statements. But it would be a fallacy to believe that the establishment of a free market for knowledge would constitute a radical alternative in education.

The establishment of a free market would indeed abolish what I have previously called the hidden curriculum of present schooling—its age-specific attendance at a graded curriculum. Equally, a free market would at first give the appearance of counteracting what I have called the occult foundations of a schooled society: the "immigration syndrome," the institutional monopoly of teaching, and the ritual of linear initiation. But at the same time a free market in education would provide the alchemist with innumerable hidden hands to fit each man into the multiple, tight little niches a more complex technocracy can provide.

Many decades of reliance on schooling has turned knowledge into a commodity, a marketable staple of a special kind. Knowledge is now regarded simultaneously as a first necessity and also as society's most precious currency. (The transformation of knowledge into a commodity is reflected in a corresponding transformation of language. Words that formerly functioned as verbs are becoming nouns that designate possessions. Until recently dwelling and learning and even healing designated activities. They are now usually conceived as commodities or services to be delivered. We talk about the manufacture of housing or the delivery of medical care. Men are no longer regarded fit to house or heal themselves. In such a society people come to believe that professional services are more valuable than personal care. Instead of learning how to nurse grandmother, the teen-ager learns to picket the hospital that does not admit her.) This attitude could easily survive the disestablishment of school, just as affiliation with a church remained a condition for office long after the adoption of the First Amendment. It is even more evident that test batteries measuring complex knowledge-packages could easily survive the disestablishment of school—and with this would go the compulsion to obligate everybody to acquire a minimum package in the knowledge stock. The scientific measurement of each man's worth and the alchemic dream of each man's "educability to his full humanity" would finally coincide. Under the appearance of a "free" market, the global village would turn into an environmental womb where pedagogic therapists control the complex navel by which each man is nourished.

At present schools limit the teacher's competence to the classroom. They prevent him from claiming man's whole life as his domain. The demise of school will remove this restriction and give a semblance of legitimacy to the life-long pedagogical invasion of everybody's privacy. It will open the way for a scramble for "knowledge" on a free market, which would lead us toward the paradox of a vulgar, albeit seemingly egalitarian, meritocracy. Unless the concept of knowledge is transformed, the disestablishment of school will lead to a wedding between a growing meritocratic system that separates learning from certification and a society committed to provide therapy for each man until he is ripe for the gilded age.

For those who subscribe to the technocratic ethos, whatever is technically possible must be made available at least to a few whether they want it or not. Neither the privation nor the frustration of the majority counts. If cobalt treatment is possible, then the city of Tegucigalpa needs one apparatus in each of its two major hospitals, at a cost that would free an important part of the population of Honduras from parasites. If supersonic speeds are possible, then it must speed the travel of some. If the flight to Mars can be conceived, then a rationale must be found to make it appear a necessity. In the technocratic ethos poverty is modernized: Not only are old alternatives closed off by new monopolies, but the lack of necessities is also compounded by a growing spread between those services that are technologically feasible and those that are in fact available to the majority.

A teacher turns "educator" when he adopts this technocratic ethos. He then acts as if education were a technological enterprise designed to make man fit into whatever environment the "progress" of science creates. He seems blind to the evidence that constant obsolescence of all commodities comes at a high price: the mounting cost of training people to know about them. He seems to forget that the rising cost of tools is purchased at a high price in education: They decrease the labor intensity of the economy, make learning on the job impossible or, at best, a privilege for a few. All over the world the cost of educating men for society rises faster than the productivity of the entire economy, and fewer people have a sense of intelligent participation in the commonweal.

A revolution against those forms of privilege and power, which are based on claims to professional knowledge, must start with a transformation of consciousness about the nature of learning. This means, above all, a shift of responsibility for teaching and learning. Knowledge can be defined as a commodity only as long as it is viewed as the result of institutional enterprise or as the fulfillment of institutional objectives. Only when a man recovers the sense of personal responsibility for what he learns and teaches can this spell be broken and the alienation of learning from living be overcome.

The recovery of the power to learn or to teach means that the teacher who takes the risk of interfering in somebody else's private affairs also assumes responsibility for the results. Similarly, the student who exposes himself to the influence of a teacher must take responsibility for his own education. For such purposes educational institutions—if they are at all needed—ideally take the form of facility centers where one can get a roof of the right size over his head, access to a piano or a kiln, and to records, books, or slides. Schools, TV stations, theaters, and the like are designed primarily for use by professionals. Deschooling society means above all the denial of professional status for the second-oldest profession, namely teaching. The certification of teachers now constitutes an undue restriction of the right to free speech: the corporate structure and professional pretensions of journalism an undue restriction on the right to free press. Compulsory attendance rules interfere with free assembly. The deschooling of society is nothing less than a cultural mutation by which a people recovers the effective use of its Constitutional freedoms: learning and teaching by men who know that they are both free rather than treated to freedom. Most people learn most of the time when they do whatever they enjoy; most people are curious and want to give meaning to whatever they come in contact with; and most people are capable of personal intimate intercourse with others unless they are stupefied by inhuman work or turned off by schooling.

The fact that people in rich countries do not learn much on their own constitutes no proof to the contrary. Rather it is a consequence of life in an environment from which, paradoxically, they cannot learn much, precisely because it is so highly programed. They are constantly frustrated by the structure of contemporary society in which the facts on which decisions can be made have become elusive. They live in an environment in which tools that can be used for creative purposes have become luxuries, an environment in which channels of communication serve a few to talk to many.

A modern myth would make us believe that the sense of impotence with which most men live today is a consequence of technology that cannot but create huge systems. But it is not technology that makes systems huge, tools immensely powerful, channels of communication one-directional. Quite the contrary: Properly controlled, technology could provide each man with the ability to understand his environment better, to shape it powerfully with his own hands, and to permit him full intercommunication to a degree never before possible. Such an alternative use of technology constitutes the central alternative in education.

If a person is to grow up he needs, first of all, access to things, to places and to processes, to events and to records. He needs to see, to touch, to tinker with, to grasp whatever there is in a meaningful setting. This access is now largely denied. When knowledge became a commodity, it acquired the protections of private property, and thus a principle designed to guard personal intimacy became a rationale for declaring facts off limits for people without the proper credentials. In schools teachers keep knowledge to themselves unless it fits into the day's program. The media inform, but exclude those things they regard as unfit to print. Information is locked into special languages, and specialized teachers live off its retranslation. Patents are protected by corporations, secrets are guarded by bureaucracies, and the power to keep others out of private preserves—be they cockpits, law offices, junkyards, or clinics—is jealously guarded by professions, institutions, and nations. Neither the political nor the professional structure of our societies, East and West, could withstand the elimination of the power to keep entire classes of people from facts that could serve them. The access to facts that I advocate goes far beyond truth in labeling. Access must be built into reality, while all we ask from advertising is a guarantee that it does not mislead. Access to reality constitutes a fundamental alternative in education to a system that only purports to teach *about* it.

Abolishing the right to corporate secrecy—even when professional opinion holds that this secrecy serves the common good—is, as shall presently appear, a much more radical political goal than the traditional demand for public ownership or control of the tools of production. The socialization of tools without the effective socialization of know-how in their use tends to put the knowledge-capitalist into the position formerly held by the financier. The technocrat's only claim to power is the stock he holds in some class of scarce and secret knowledge, and the best means to protect its value is a large and capital-intensive organization that renders access to know-how formidable and forbidding.

It does not take much time for the interested learner to acquire almost any skill that he wants to use. We tend to forget this in a society where professional teachers monopolize entrance into all fields, and thereby stamp teaching by uncertified individuals as quackery. There are few mechanical skills used in industry or research that are as demanding, complex, and dangerous as driving cars, a skill that most people quickly acquire from a peer. Not all people are suited for advanced logic, yet those who are make rapid progress if they are challenged to play mathematical games at an early age. One out of twenty kids in Cuernavaca can beat me at Wiff 'n' Proof after a couple of weeks' training. In four months all but a small percentage of motivated adults at our CIDOC center learn Spanish well enough to conduct academic business in the new language.

A first step toward opening up access to skills would be to provide various incentives for skilled individuals to share their knowledge. Inevitably, this would run counter to the interest of guilds and professions and unions. Yet, multiple apprenticeship is attractive: It provides everybody with an opportunity to learn something about almost anything. There is no reason why a person should not combine the ability to drive a car, repair telephones and toilets, act as a midwife, and function as an architectural draftsman. Special-interest groups and their disciplined consumers would, of course, claim that the public needs the protection of a professional guarantee. But this argument is now steadily being challenged by consumer protection associations. We have to take much more seriously the objection that economists raise to the radical socialization of skills: that "progress" will be impeded if knowledge—patents, skills, and all the rest—is democratized. Their argument can be faced only if we demonstrate to them the growth rate of futile diseconomies generated by any existing educational system.

Access to people willing to share their skills is no guarantee of learning. Such access is restricted not only by the monopoly of educational programs over learning and of unions over licensing but also by a technology of scarcity. The skills that count today are know-how in the use of highly specialized tools that were designed to be scarce. These tools produce goods or render services that everybody wants but only a few can enjoy, and which only a limited number of people know how to use. Only a few privileged individuals out of the total number of people who have a given disease ever benefit from the results of sophisticated medical technology, and even fewer doctors develop the skill to use it.

The same results of medical research have, however, also been employed to create a basic medical tool kit that permits Army and Navy medics, with only a few months of training, to obtain results, under battlefield conditions, that would have been beyond the expectations of full-fledged doctors during World War II. On an even simpler level any peasant girl could learn how to diagnose and treat most infections if medical scientists prepared dosages and instructions specifically for a given geographic area.

All these examples illustrate the fact that educational considerations alone suffice to demand a radical reduction of the professional structure that now impedes the mutual relationship between the scientist and the majority of people who want access to science. If this demand were heeded, all men could learn to use yesterday's tools, rendered more effective and durable by modern science, to create tomorrow's world.

Unfortunately, precisely the contrary trend prevails at present. I know a coastal area in South America where most people support themselves by fishing from small boats. The outboard motor is certainly the tool that has changed most dramatically the lives of these coastal fishermen. But in the area I have surveyed, half of all outboard motors that were purchased between 1945 and 1950 are still kept running by constant tinkering, while half the motors purchased in 1965 no longer run because they were not built to be repaired. Technological progress provides the majority of people with gadgets they cannot afford and deprives them of the simpler tools they need.

Metals, plastics, and ferro cement used in building have greatly improved since the 1940s and ought to provide more people the opportunity to create their own homes. But while in the United States, in 1948, more than 30 percent of all one-family homes were owner-built, by the end of the 1960s the percentage of those who acted as their own contractors had dropped to less than 20 percent.

The lowering of the skill level through so-called economic development becomes even more visible in Latin America. Here most people still build their own homes from floor to roof. Often they use mud, in the form of adobe, and thatchwork of unsurpassed utility in the moist, hot, and windy climate. In other places they make their dwellings out of cardboard, oil-drums, and other industrial refuse. Instead of providing people with simple tools and highly standardized, durable, and easily repaired components, all governments have gone in for the mass production of low-cost buildings. It is clear that not one single country can afford to provide satisfactory modern dwelling units for the majority of its people. Yet, everywhere this policy makes it progressively more difficult for the majority to acquire the knowledge and skills they need to build better houses for themselves.

Educational considerations permit us to formulate a second fundamental characteristic that any post-industrial society must possess: a basic tool kit that by its very nature counteracts technocratic control. For educational reasons we must work toward a society in which scientific knowledge is incorporated in tools and components that can be used meaningfully in units small enough to be within the reach of all. Only such tools can socialize access to skills. Only such tools favor temporary associations among those who want to use them for a specific occasion. Only such tools allow specific goals to emerge in the process of their use, as any tinkerer knows. Only the combination of guaranteed access to facts and of limited power in most tools renders it possible to envisage a subsistence economy capable of incorporating the fruits of modern science.

The development of such a scientific subsistence economy is unquestionably to the advantage of the overwhelming majority of all people in poor countries. It is also the only alternative to progressive pollution, exploitation, and opaqueness in rich countries. But, as we have seen, the dethroning of the GNP cannot be achieved, without simultaneously subverting GNE (Gross National Education—usually conceived as manpower capitalization). An egalitarian economy cannot exist in a society in which the right to produce is conferred by schools.

The feasibility of a modern subsistence economy does not depend on new scientific inventions. It depends primarily on the ability of a society to agree on fundamental, self-chosen anti-bureaucratic and anti-technocratic restraints.

These restraints can take many forms, but they will not work unless they touch the basic dimensions of life. (The decision of Congress against development of the supersonic transport plane is one of the most encouraging steps in the right direction.) The substance of these voluntary social restraints would be very simple matters that can be fully understood and judged by any prudent man. The issues at stake in the SST controversy provide a good example. All such restraints would be chosen to promote stable and equal enjoyment of scientific know-how. The French say that it takes a thousand years to educate a peasant to deal with a cow. It would not take two generations to help all people in Latin America or Africa to use and repair outboard motors, simple cars, pumps, medicine kits, and ferro cement machines if their design does not change every few years. And since a joyful life is one of constant meaningful intercourse with others in a meaningful environment, equal enjoyment does translate into equal education.

At present a consensus on austerity is difficult to imagine. The reason usually given for the impotence of the majority is stated in terms of political or economic class. What is not usually understood is that the new class structure of a schooled society is even more powerfully controlled by vested interests. No doubt an imperialist and capitalist organization of society provides the social structure within which a minority can have disproportionate influence over the effective opinion of the majority. But in a technocratic society the power of a minority of knowledge capitalists can prevent the formation of true public opinion through control of scientific know-how and the media of communication. Constitutional guarantees of free speech, free press, and free assembly were meant to ensure government by the people. Modern electronics, photo-offset presses, time-sharing computers, and telephones have in principle provided the hardware that could give an entirely new meaning to these freedoms. Unfortunately, these things are used in modern media to increase the power of knowledge-bankers to funnel their program-packages through international chains to more people, instead of being used to increase true networks that provide equal opportunity for encounter among the members of the majority.

Deschooling the culture and social structure requires the use of technology to make participatory politics possible. Only on the basis of a majority coalition can limits to secrecy and growing power be determined without dictatorship. We need a new environment in which growing up can be classless, or we will get a brave new world in which Big Brother educates us all.

PUBLIC SCHOOL REFORM: THE OPEN CLASSROOM

The idea of deschooling takes us, in theory, past schools of any kind, past even free schools, but in terms of fact, the schools themselves are very much with us, and the young are still in them, and what then is to be done?

That is the question which has confronted well-meaning parents and teachers for the past several years, and it is the question which the essays in this section set out to answer. Because it is a difficult question for which there are no easy answers, these essays raise as many questions as they answer. The most important question, perhaps, is whether or not the kinds of freedom and community which are available through free schools or deschooling can be established in public schools. In some places, for instance, radically innovative experiments like the Parkway Project in Philadelphia have been set up. But for the most part such experiments have been short-lived. Measured by the ordinary standards at work in public education, they are disorderly and inefficient, and despite the fact that they are not nearly as radical as most free schools, they still meet with strong community opposition and parental anxiety. For that reason the liberalization of public schools is usually limited to changes in dress and conduct codes, the provision of a wider range of courses and the occasional establishment of "schools-within-schools" for the most restless or dissatisfied students.

But such changes are surface changes only, and if the ideas at work in the radical education movement have made their way into the schools in any deeply felt way, they have probably done so most fully in the form of the "open classroom." Originally patterned on the model of the English Primary School, the open classroom has come to represent for many parents and teachers an ideal kind of freedom: the creation of a wider sense of choice and the diminishment of coercion within the ordinary limits of the public schools.

Whether that kind of change corresponds to the kind of freedom free-schoolers and deschoolers are after, or whether it will really catch on in the schools, are still open questions. Certainly there is a big difference between the kinds of communal participation envisioned by free-schoolers, or the exhilarated self-direction of the deschoolers, and the institutionalized, ritualized virtues of the open classroom. In some ways those virtues are like prison reform: long overdue and better than what they replace, but still too little and too late, leaving untouched most of the things wrong with schooling.

In the essays which follow John Holt and Herbert Kohl, two of the leading spokesmen for school reform, examine the ways in which the open classroom can be put to use in the schools. Unlike most proponents of the open classroom (whose allegiance is usually to the school system *as a system*), Holt and Kohl are at best ambivalent about public schooling, and both of them have elsewhere argued as strongly as Illich or Goodman that the schools must be replaced by something else altogether. Kohl, who began as a teacher in the Harlem public schools (and wrote about it in *Thirty-six Children*) later established in Berkeley an alternative school for ghetto teenagers called Other Ways, which was precisely that: an alternative to public schooling. And Holt, who has become more radical with every book he writes, accepts in *Freedom and Beyond,* one of his latest books, most of Illich's arguments about deschooling.

But despite those attitudes, both Kohl and Holt are moved in these essays to try to convince people to make changes in the schools. They do not do that because such changes will revive or save the school system. Instead, moved by the facts of life and a kind of resigned pragmatism, they seem merely to want to make the schools less destructive and more tolerable for the students trapped in them. Where most open classroom enthusiasts (see Charles Silberman's book, *Crisis in The Classroom*) feel that they know precisely what to do (that is, the best of possible alternatives), Holt and Kohl suggest what they do because they don't know what else to do. They reduce in scope and size their original visions of education, as if hoping in that way to make them more practicable and acceptable and therefore of immediate use to the young.

But does that work? There is as yet no clear indication that it does. The problem is that so much is lost in that process of reduction that what remains—even if acceptable—may leave the schools fundamentally unchanged. Though the open classroom clearly makes schools more tolerable for children, nothing much about it challenges the traditional approaches or effects of the school as a *system,* and that may mean that the idea of the open classroom does not push us far enough in the direction of new thought or activity.

It is precisely that issue which makes the essays which follow important. Their significance lies in the fact that they raise the question of what is and is not possible in the public schools—and they also provide a way for some teachers to find that out.

not trust us or believe us. Given their experience, they are quite
not to. A student in a traditional school learns before long in a
hundred different ways that the school is not on his side; that it is working, not for him, but for the community and the state; that it is not interested in him except as he serves its purposes; and that among all the reasons for which the adults in the school do things, his happiness, health, and growth are by far the least important. He has probably also learned that most of the adults in the school do not tell him the truth and indeed are not allowed to—unless they are willing to run the risk of being fired, which most of them are not. They are not independent and responsible persons, free to say what they think, feel, believe, or to do what seems reasonable and right. They are employees and spokesmen, telling the children whatever the school administration, the school board, the community, or the legislature want the children to be told. Their job by whatever means they can to "motivate" the students to do whatever the school wants. So, when a school or teacher says that the students don't have to play the old school game anymore, most of them, certainly those who have not been "good students," will not believe it. They would be foolish if they did.

We must try to understand and accept this, without getting hurt feelings or taking it as some very personal kind of rejection. This may be far from easy. A school, or teachers, or teacher, that offers students very much choice has probably gone to some trouble to be able to do so, and even risk—risk of misunderstanding or hostility from parents or community or fellow-teachers. If after we have run this risk to give students more freedom, choice, and control in their learning, they show us that they do not believe or trust us, we may be tempted to think "Well, you aren't worth going to this trouble for in the first place, the hell with you, we'll go on doing things in here the old way if that is what you want." But we must resist this temptation, and keep our offer of freedom and choice out on the table even though at first it is not believed or used. It might be helpful, if we feel comfortable doing it, to say to the students that we understand their skepticism and suspicion, and the reasons for it, and are sympathetic rather than hurt or angry. We might even invite them to talk about their reactions to our offer. On the other hand, if students do not believe our offer they may not trust enough to talk candidly about their reasons for not believing it. Also, they may not really know, well enough to put it into words, why they disbelieve it or are afraid to make use of it.

Some may think that in all this talk of trusting and not trusting I am cynical, making complications where none exist. In some cases, they may be right. There are many schools and classes in which the students, given this chance to plan and direct their own learning and growth, have seen it right away for a good thing and have wasted no time in

JOHN HOLT

The Problem of Choi[ce]

Teachers very often say to me, "Suppose we tell kids th[ey have] the freedom to choose what they are going to study, an[d how] they are going to study it, and they don't choose an[ything,] anything? Then what do we do?" A good many teacher[s trying] to open up their classrooms, usually in a junior hig[h] school, have said that this has in fact happened.

First, we should try to see this situation through the e[yes of the student.] For years he has been playing a school game which l[ooks] like this. The teacher holds up a hoop and says "Jump[!"] if he makes it, he gets a doggy biscuit. Then the teache[r holds it a] little higher and again says "Jump!" Another jump, a[nd] perhaps the student makes a feeble pretense of jum[ping. "I'm] jumping as high as I can, this is the best I can do." [Or he sits on] the floor and refuse to jump. But in any case the rul[es are] simple and clear—hoop, jump, biscuit. Now along co[mes a teacher who] says, "We aren't going to play that game anymor[e. You] decide for yourselves what you're going to do." What [is the student going] to think about this? Almost certainly, he is going to t[hink, "It's about find-] ing the hoop! It was bad enough having to jump thr[ough the hoop, but] now I have to find it." Then after a while he is li[kely to think, "On] second thought, maybe I don't have to find it. If I ju[st sit tight,] pretty soon that hoop is going to slip out of its hid[ing place, and] we'll be back to the old game where at least I kno[w how to be] comfortable."

In short, if we make this offer of freedom, choice, [to stu-]dents who have spent much time in traditional sc[hools,]

From *Freedom and Beyond* by John Holt. Copyright © 1972
by E. P. Dutton & Co., Inc. and used with their permission.

87

making good use of it. If only it could be this way everywhere. But from experience we know that it often has not been and is often not going to be. For one thing, in offering freedom and choice to students, we may be trusting them less than we think. Many parents, and more than a few educators, have seized on the idea of the open classroom, freedom, and choice, not as a way of having students direct their own learning, explore the world in the way that seems best to them, but only as a way of getting them to do conventional schoolwork more willingly and hence more rapidly than before. In short, they believe in freedom only as a "motivating" device. This is a cruel deception, bound to lead us to disappointment. If we have such an idea anywhere in our minds, students will be aware of it, even if we are not. They will see the offer as not being real. They will know that the old hoop is still there, but hidden.

Not long ago I saw a vivid example of this. I was invited to a conference, held in a new high school, built only a few years before at great expense, and already quite famous. The school, like most, was too big, too elaborate, too inflexible, and too ponderous. Handsome enough in its way, but without color, humor, warmth, or grace. Why do we think that humane learning can go on in buildings that look as if they were designed to hold atomic secrets? Inside, the usual bare walls, unrelieved by any decoration or human touch. The big talking point of the school was that it had been designed for a program in which the students would do a great deal of independent learning. Instead of the usual classrooms, there were a number of resource areas and centers—in Mathematics, Physical Sciences, History, and so forth. The idea was that students would have a great deal of unscheduled time that they would be free to use as they wished, going to this or that center. Though the program was only in its second year, we were told it was "not working." The students were not making good use of their time, it was said, just loafing around talking to each other. The school had to cut back on the unscheduled time and schedule more regular classes—for which the building was not well designed.

One student spoke mournfully to me about this. He had two or three very strong interests—photography, writing, and something else. He said, "Last year I had a lot of time, I could really get into these things. This year they have taken more than half of it away, and they'll probably take more away next year. But already my day is so chopped up with classes that I can't really do any serious projects in the darkroom. I might as well forget it." I asked him why the school had changed. He said, "Of course, a lot of the kids weren't doing much of anything. But they didn't give us time to find out what we might want to do. I already knew what I wanted. Most of them didn't. But at least you'd think that they'd let the students who were making good use of the program go on doing what they were interested in. But I can't get out of classes even to do projects. I have to go like everyone else. In another year or two this will just be like any other school."

If the school was sincere in its offer to the students, it was unwise to have lost heart so quickly. What would probably have happened, if they had let it, if they had had the patience to wait for it, is that more and more students, like the one I talked to, would have found things to do that they could put their whole energy into, and that gradually more and more students would have learned about this, followed their example, or been drawn into their activities. Young people naturally like to share what gives them real pleasure and satisfaction. My student friend's interest in photography would certainly in time have touched and enriched the lives of other students. But the school did not allow this to happen.

At another time during the day I was being shown around the school by someone who knew it. We went by one of the biology resources centers. It was lavishly equipped, but with few of the signs—human junk, stuff brought in, bones, skulls, skins, nests, shells—of a place where people really care about what they are doing. Five or six boys and girls were sitting in a group in the middle of the room, talking. My guide looked at them for a while through the door. Then, as we moved away, he said to me sourly, "Doesn't look to me as if they're doing much biology." In his voice there was a world of suspicion and contempt. Worse yet, satisfaction—I knew those kids were no good, and they're proving I'm right. I said mildly that for all we knew they might be talking about biology. He made no comment. I let the matter drop. What seems clear to me even now is that students must from the very first have read and understood the secret feelings of this man and perhaps many others like him. Perhaps they knew that in this school, resource centers or no, they were never really going to be allowed to learn and talk about what really mattered to them. Small wonder most of them decided to escape from the usual grind for whatever time they could.

But lack of trust in us is not the only reason why students may be slow to use the freedom and choice we offer them. Suppose we get over this first hump, and the students believe our offer is genuine. The next problem is that they may not trust themselves enough to be willing to choose. We must not be surprised at this either. They have been taught in school to distrust themselves, and they have learned. It is one of the few things that schools teach well. Everything the traditional school does says clearly to the student that he cannot be trusted to do anything, not even to make the simplest choices about what he will learn or do next or how he will do it. Nothing is left to chance or the student's own design.

To choose is to risk. Faced with a choice, the student may well think, if I have to decide what I'm going to do, how do I know that I will like it or get anything out of it. The choice may be no good. But then I'll have no one else to blame. I can't say, as at least I can if I mess up regular schoolwork, that it was the teacher's fault for asking an unfair question, or not telling me what she really wanted, or not teaching me what I was supposed to know. There is nobody to blame but me. If I fail, it will be my fault. This is too much for most children. They learn in school—another one of the few things they really do learn—that since to fail is the worst thing of all, it is best to take no chances. We must realize that when we ask or invite them to make choices we are asking them to take a risk much larger than the risks we have spent years teaching them never to take. No wonder many of them hang back. This too may be something it would be helpful to talk about.

It is not just the people we call children who find choosing difficult. A few years ago I taught at the Harvard Graduate School of Education a one-semester course called Student-Directed Learning—which came to be called T-52, its number in the catalog. Many of the students were in their early twenties, still on the schooling ladder, but many others were experienced teachers and school administrators, some as old as I was or older. At our first meeting I talked a while about how I saw the course, what I planned to do in it. I had a certain amount of resources and experiences, all having to do with student-directed or open learning, that I was going to put before them. I would talk and lead some class discussions; I had some other people coming in; the class was welcome to find and bring in people of their own. I had some films to show them of alternative schools already at work. I had a list of books and articles about open learning that had seemed to me useful, that I liked, and that I strongly recommended. If they were interested in and wanted to find out more about anything on the list, I would be glad to tell them. I also had a list of places in the area where, in different ways, student-directed learning was going on, and I encouraged them to visit such places, spend as much time there as they wanted and could arrange, and get involved in any way that might seem useful. I also said that the course was Pass-Fail, that everyone enrolled would get a Pass, that there would be no exams or compulsory written work, that attendance at class sessions was optional.

I urged them to keep a private journal or notes, in whatever form they liked, of thoughts or reactions or observations that came up in the course of their work, inside class or out. I said that I would be very glad to read any such writing that they wanted to share with me. I said that if anyone has some ideas that he wanted to give to everyone, I would give him a ditto stencil, he could write his piece on this, and I would make copies for the whole class. I suggested that we might make up a kind of open journal, rather like the correspondence columns of some British newspapers, and magazines, in which they could write whatever thoughts they wanted others to hear, or respond in various ways to what other people had written. I said that as I found new articles, newspaper stories, or interesting material, I would post them on the walls of the classroom, and invited others to do the same—to use the walls as a kind of open bulletin board. I was full of bright ideas and suggestions.

But having proposed all this, I said that none of this was required. Here were these resources on Student-Directed Learning. They could use all of it, or any parts of it they wished, or substitute something else of their own choosing, or do nothing whatever. The class seemed satisfied with this; indeed, they shouted down one young angry who said that I was dominating the class, and why did they have to sit around and listen to what this guy Holt said, why couldn't they just get themselves together? Why did they have to sit in the chairs in this lecture hall? I said they didn't; sit on the floor or the lecturer's platform, if you like. They all came and sat on the platform. Next class they were back in the chairs—and why not, they were more comfortable.

Anyway, the class seemed to think my offer and plan were reasonable. We went along smoothly enough for six weeks or so. Nobody did any writing, nobody put anything in the journal, nobody took up most of those bright ideas. But the class sessions seemed interesting, and I knew some things were happening outside. Then at one class meeting there was an explosion. Many people in the class began to attack me about the course. They were very angry. You don't care what we think! You never tell us to write anything! You're not interested in our ideas! I repeated the suggestions and offers I had made at the beginning of the course. They said, You'd don't care about us, *otherwise you'd tell us what to do.* I said I did care about them, that was why I didn't want to tell them what to do. If it was true, and it seemed to be, that many of them had never had the chance to decide for themselves whether to read a book or not, write a paper or not, go to a meeting or not, then I thought it was time they decided.

Later, one of the students sympathetic to me told me about the book problem. He said, "You've no idea what a bind you put us in. Here are all these books on your list. You say they are good, and on the whole we believe you. We'd like to read them. But they are not required, we're not going to be tested on them, and meanwhile here is all this other stuff we have to do at the Ed School, more reading than we can ever get finished, a lot of it probably not as good as the stuff on your list. But those other courses are graded, and we need those grades. So we'd better read those required books and let these books go. Then we think, 'But Holt says they are good books, and I'll bet they are, I'd like to read them.' 'But I haven't got the time!' 'But it's not fair to Holt not to read any of his reading stuff just because he said we didn't have to!' 'Not fair, hell! He *said* we didn't have to.' 'Yes, but . . . but . . .' The more we think about it, the more guilty we feel for not reading those books, and the madder we get at you for making us feel so guilty." He said all this in a good-natured way, and I laughed, and said I was sorry to make life so difficult, and I hoped someday he might read some of those books.

Part of the point here may be that it doesn't take much sense to talk of "giving freedom" to people. The most we can do is put within reach certain choices, and remove certain coercions and constraints. Whether doing this creates for other people something they sense as release, liberation, opportunity, freedom, or whether it just puts them in a more painful spot than ever, is very much up to them and how they see things. There isn't much we can do to control it. We have to assume, or at least I choose to, that in the long run more choices and fewer constraints, less coercion, less fear, is good for most people—if only because it gives them a chance to look for and maybe find something that they really want.

Well, we went round and round about this in class. I don't think I converted everyone. Some of the people who were mad stayed mad. Some people just left the class without saying anything. Some of them, perhaps, needed the time to work for those grades in those other courses, or simply to think about things, or amuse themselves, or sleep. More power to them. Some people were glad to grab the easy credit. Enough of the class stayed with me, and took an increasingly active part in it, including running it, to make me feel—as I wanted to feel—that my effort was worth making. Except that I might do more to prepare people for the anxiety of choosing, in the same circumstances I would probably do things very much the same way again.

Another problem for these nonchoosers may be that they do not know what there is to choose from, what choices are possible. Perhaps none of the choices available may appeal to them. All too often teachers or schools say to children, "Now you can do anything you want," when in fact there is nothing to do. Once I visited an elementary school class run by a very nice young man. He had heard about the British style open classrooms and the integrated day and was trying to introduce them in his room. He couldn't figure out why the children didn't seem to want to do anything but run around and bother each other. I looked around the room. Nothing there but the traditional classroom junk—basal readers, workbooks, texts. No games, puzzles, tools, equipment; no typewriter, camera, tape recorder, music stuff, science stuff; no art supplies, not even good magazines or books. As tactfully as I could I tried to suggest that it wasn't much help to tell the children they could do what they wanted if there was in fact almost nothing for them *to* do. He saw my point, and we began to talk about some of the kinds of things that he might bring into the class, or projects he might get going.

If it is frustrating to be told to choose when there is nothing to choose from, it may be frightening, confusing, and paralyzing to have too much to choose from, like a child in a huge toy store. Even in well-established open classrooms, comfortable in the integrated day, it may be wiser not to have all the available equipment and material in the room at the same time. It clutters up the room and makes a major problem of putting things away and keeping some kind of order. Also, if something is under their noses too long, children may no longer notice it. What is too familiar becomes invisible. It would be sensible, if a given piece of equipment has not been used in some time, to take it out of the class without saying anything, store it, and then, after a while, bring it back. Perhaps seeing it after an absence, the children will notice it and be interested in it.

When we first try to open up our classrooms it may make the change easier for everyone if instead of offering a wide choice from the start, we widen the range of choice very gradually. If we say to a student used to traditional classes, "Now you may choose to do anything you want," he may do nothing. If instead we say, "You can choose between these two or three possibilities," he may be more able to choose. Next time we can offer four or five choices. When students seem comfortable with this we can say, "Choose between any of these, or if none of them suits you, substitute a choice of your own." Thus we may change so smoothly from formal class and teacher-directed learning to open class and learner-directed learning that the students will not be threatened by it.

When I taught my last fifth-grade class, I began the year with a fairly traditional class structure, the day divided into periods, schedule written on the board. The schedule wasn't very tight and we didn't stick to it to the minute, but it was there. Soon I introduced what I called a read or work period. In this students could read whatever they wanted, or do any other kind of schoolwork they wanted. Very gradually we began to push out the boundaries of this period. It was the students' idea as much as my own. Someone would say, "Can I draw a picture, or do a puzzle, or write a letter?" I would say Yes. So these became OK activities. Later, someone might ask such things as, "Can I play checkers, or chess, with so-and-so? Or, Can I talk with so-and-so into the tape recorder? Or, Can I listen to some music over the phones? Or, Can so-and-so and I have a conversation?" I would say, fine, if you can do it quietly enough not to bother other people. Most of the time, they could. And so we developed the free period. It was less useful than it might have been; I had not yet visited the British primary schools, and had far less in the way of materials and projects than I would have had a few years later. But it was still the best part of the school day. More and more, the children themselves would ask for a free period, not just to have a chance to do nothing, but because there was something they wanted to do. Sometimes they would ask for a straight read or work period, or a quiet free period.

I see now, though I didn't then, that I might have used the same gradual method to open up the physical arrangement of the class. I was still stuck with the idea that the desks had to be in rows. Every so often

I would say that the children could swap places with someone else, or make any new arrangement that was agreeable to all parties, and several times I moved my own desk to a new part of the room to give the whole class a fresh outlook. Even such minor changes as these seemed stimulating to the class, as if with the desks in a new place many new things might be possible.

Often, when I describe to teachers or would-be teachers this fifth-grade class and the way I gradually made it more open, someone will say that since I still controlled the class and the choices, and since the students still could not do anything that I did not approve, the class was really no different from conventional classes, and its seeming openness was a fake. There is some truth in this. It never occurred to me that it might be a good idea to give up my control of the class, and I would not have been allowed to even had I wanted. The students and I knew that their range of choices was limited by what I or the school would approve, and we did not pretend otherwise. One day when I announced a free period and said they could do what they wanted, one boy asked, "Can I go home?" The children all laughed. I apologized for careless speech and said, No he could not, when I said they could do anything they wanted I meant provided it was within the classroom and did not disturb the rest of the building. But he knew that before he asked. As a matter of fact, I suspect that he was at least as happy in that class as he was at home, and that given a real choice of going home he would not have gone. I don't think the children felt that the class was basically like the ones they had been used to, or that their choices were not real because not unlimited.

Finding interesting things for children to do is not too difficult, if they have not been in school too long, or have not been made to feel, by being tracked and labeled, that they are unusually stupid or worthless. We can easily buy, borrow, or salvage many kinds of materials that will be interesting in many ways to young children. We can invent many projects that many of them will find interesting, and they can invent many more themselves. For older children the task may be harder, for many reasons. If they have interests or hobbies, they may need more specialized or expensive equipment than the school has or can afford. They may be more bored, more distrustful, more ashamed of their own curiosity and ignorance, more unwilling to expose themselves and their interests to adults or even their peers.

In this connection I think of a question I am often asked by teachers, sometimes in a tone of bafflement and concern, all too often in a tone of anger and contempt—"What do you do with the student who isn't interested in anything?" First of all, there is no such person. Everyone alive is interested in something, if only himself—and usually much more than that. We might say of a student that he doesn't *appear* to be interested in anything, or at least any of the things we try to interest him in. But this only means that he has chosen not to let us see his interests, perhaps because he has learned from experience that the less the adults, teachers above all, know about what he cares about, the safer he is from mockery, contempt, put-downs. He has learned to put barriers between himself and us, and to wear a mask of elaborate indifference, unconcern, and disdain. But this mask is not the person. Behind the mask and the barriers is the true person, full of fear, shame, self-hatred, self-contempt. Afraid of the world, he uses all his energy to protect himself against it. But this protection comes at terrible cost to himself, for all these strategies of deliberate failure, incompetence, withdrawal, and resistance only add to his sense of shame and worthlessness.

We cannot leap over those barriers, or break through them, or force them down. They can be raised as high and made as strong as they need to be, and they can only be lowered from inside. The question becomes, how do we help that person inside to become less afraid? Sometimes it may help to talk about his fear, or anxiety, though it is probably true that at least some of the barriers will have to be lowered even before such a talk could take place. But many fearful people, particularly boys from low-income cultures, would rather die than admit that they were afraid. Perhaps with such boys it might be more helpful not to talk at all of fear or being afraid, but instead talk as concretely as possible about things they expect to happen that they don't want to happen—for if we are afraid, we are almost always afraid *of something*, and the more clearly we can see what it is we are afraid of, the more likely we are to be able to cope with that fear.

It is no help at all to tell people who are afraid that their fears are groundless, that there is nothing to be afraid of, or that what they're afraid of won't hurt them. It is a little like telling someone who fears that a dog may bite him, "Don't be silly, that dog won't bite, unless he thinks you're afraid of him." When we dismiss someone's fears as foolish and groundless, we only make him more afraid. "They don't understand," he thinks. "They don't even *see* the danger. Because they don't see it, they may try to 'help' me by pushing me into it." We have to accept people's fears as real, as being caused not by their imaginations but by their experience. In R. D. Laing's phrase, we must not "invalidate their experience." What we can do is to try in every way not to add to their fears, not to give them new reasons for being fearful. It is like the old fable of the Sun and the Wind, trying to see who could make the traveler take off his cloak. The Wind tried to blow it off by main force, but the harder he blew, the tighter the man wrapped the cloak around him. The Sun in his turn beamed his rays down on the man until he was so warm that he took off his cloak. The way to get people to lower their barriers is to create as much as we can a situation in which they feel no need for them.

One way to get the student to come out from hiding, is to do all we can to legitimize his interests. In other words, to make him feel that whatever he is interested in is OK, a perfectly good place from which to look at and begin to explore the world, as good as any other, indeed better than any other. We will not make him feel this unless we understand ourselves that it is true. This will be hard for people who have for years been misschooled into thinking that life, the world, human experience, are divided up into disciplines or subjects or bodies of knowledge, some of them serious, noble, important, others ignoble and trivial. It is not so. The world and human experience are one whole. There are no dotted lines in it separating History from Geography or Mathematics from Science or Chemistry from Physics. In fact, *out there,* there are no such things as History or Geography or Chemistry or Physics. Out there is—out there. But the world, the universe, human experience, are vast. We can't take them in all at once. So we choose, sensibly enough, to look at this part of reality, or that; to ask this kind of question about it, or that. If we look at one part, in one way, and ask one kind of question, we may be thinking like a historian; if we look at another part, ask another question, we may be thinking like a physicist, or a chemist, or a psychologist, or a philosopher. But these different ways of looking at reality should not make us forget that it is all one piece, and that from any one place in it we can get to all the other places.

Teachers have often asked me, and always with contempt, "What do we do with a kid who is only interested in hot rods?" Nobody is *only* interested in hot rods. But let's agree that he is mainly interested in them. What's wrong with that? A hot rod is an automobile, and in all of man's history few inventions have done so much to change the whole shape of human life, and indeed the face of the earth itself. It has greatly changed, and in many ways seriously damaged, our cities. It has created the suburb, and so doing destroyed much of the country. Some people (including me) think that it is one of the most destructive of all man's inventions. It has enormously changed the ways in which we live, work, spend money, and amuse ourselves. Also, it is a machine, and so embodies Physics, Chemistry, Thermodynamics, Metallurgy, and so on. It takes a great many men and enormously complicated machines to make it. Indeed, it probably did more than any other single product to advance the techniques of modern mass production. Both as an invention, and as an economic product, it has a history. How did men come to invent it? By what steps did they perfect it? How was it first manufactured and marketed? How did today's enormous automobile companies grow into being?

One teacher said, after I had posed some of the questions above, "But how is all this going to help him make a living?" Strictly from the point of view of money, everything that a kid, especially a poor kid, learns messing around with hot rods will probably be worth more than most of what he is told to study in high school. And any young person who out of curiosity begins to find out all he can about the automobile and the many ways in which it affects other aspects of our life and society will have enough to keep him busy for a long time. Someday he may be better able than most conventionally schooled experts to think of ways to tame the automobile, to make it less destructive and more humane and useful—itself one of the urgent problems of our time.

At another time someone asked—not angrily, because pottery is more respectable than hot rods, less lower class—what to do about some kid who was "only" interested in pottery. But look at what is in pottery. Geology—how clay is made, in what sorts of places we look for it. The Physics and Chemistry and Mathematics of firing, kilns, cones, glazes. There are endless connections with History, Art, Anthropology, Archaeology.

This doesn't mean that if we find out that a student is interested in hot rods or anything else, we ought to try to make him think about all the questions I have suggested. He might be interested in hearing about them, but he should not feel that he has to do anything about them. If he wants to explore them further, good. Nor am I trying to suggest that, whatever a student may be interested in, we can always find clever ways to lure him into thinking about things that we think are more important, because they are closer to conventional school subjects. It's a great mistake to think that a young person with a strong interest in something like hot rods or football is somehow cut off from the mainstream of life, that if he thinks seriously about them he will be some sort of narrow specialist, that for the sake of breadth of learning we have to pull him away from what he cares most about. Any interest, any aspect of life, is connected to many other aspects of it and to life as a whole. Our task is to find ways in which we might help a student, who may already have been made to feel by ignorant, prejudiced, contemptuous adults that his interests were trivial, realize instead that they are not trivial, but as good a place as any other from which to look at and explore the world.

People who object to giving students in school a chance to talk to each other like to say that their talk is trivial. If it is, we have made it so by never taking them seriously, by teaching them through our indifference or active contempt not to take themselves seriously. Gail Ashby shows us this in an essay called "The Child I Was," which appears in the book, *This Book Is about Schools* (a collection of pieces, many of them excellent, from the magazine, *This Magazine Is About Schools*). In this story, and perhaps more indirectly in the film *High School,* we see how young people are cut off from and learn to fear and despise what is most real, important, and serious in themselves. We hear very clearly the effect of this in the speech of a lot of poor kids, which when not hostile, challenging, quarrelsome, is offhand, mocking, uncommitted, cynical, and full of an elaborate indifference.

I took part once in a writing class in a small, open high school, part of a larger, more conventional system. Most of the students in the class were typical of the school, upper middle class, excellent students, bound for college and probably graduate school. One boy was an exception. I might have thought him a fish out of water, except that he seemed a welcome and respected member of the group. Also, since attendance at class was not compulsory, I assume that he would not have gone had he not enjoyed it. He was of lower middle- or working-class background. When I arrived, the class had just started to read and discuss a short piece he had written. It described an almost serious accident he had had while driving too fast in a souped-up car. His story was well-written, but what struck me about it was its tone. He would not let the reader *into* the incident. He had seemed for a second close to death, and described his feelings very vividly; but every few sentences, just as his story began to take hold, he would throw in some mocking, sardonic observation altogether out of keeping with the rest of the story. They seemed to have no purpose except to say, "You know, I don't take any of this seriously, and you're a fool if you do."

We were all interested in what had happened, and encouraged the boy to talk more about it. The setting was informal; teacher, six students, and I were all jammed into a small office. His talk took us into a strange world, a world of souped-up Detroit cars—we were all foreign car snobs, Porsches and BMW's we could relate to, not 450-cubic-inch Chevys and Pontiacs—a world in which it was perfectly a commonplace amusement to get in a car, often by yourself, and just drive around, not going anywhere, at suicidal speeds. He talked freely and well and had a gift for the right word and phrase; obviously a very bright and perceptive young man. But in all his talk as in his writing there was this same mocking, stand-offish tone, the same refusal to commit or invest himself in what he was saying, to put himself into his words. Even when he seemed most involved in his story, with voice, expression, and gesture he was constantly saying, "This isn't real or important; don't take it seriously, I don't; believe it or don't believe it, I don't care either way."

Lower-income children are not the only ones who learn to feel this way. An eighth-grade private school teacher once invited me to talk to her class. On a warm spring day we sat outside on the grass and discussed what it might mean to be able to direct one's own learning, explore the world in one's own way instead of someone else's. The students were very excited, involved, and serious. They began to talk about the many ways in which adults seemed never to take their ideas and wants seriously, but always to find reasons for preventing them from doing what they most wanted. Thus, in this particular school they wanted very much to have a lounge or common room for the older students, a room of their own where they could go, meet, and talk without teachers hovering around. But the school kept putting them off, talking about not enough money, maybe in a few years, we'll think about it—all the delaying tactics that children and students everywhere know so well. (If we stall them off, they'll soon forget about it.) I suggested to them that they consider and take up with the school the possibility of building this lounge themselves. They were very excited by this, and discussed with great animation possible ways of doing this. The hour went very quickly, and they all urged me to come back a week later to talk about these things further, which I gladly agreed to do.

When I came to the classroom a week later the students were at another class. Their teacher told me that they had all discussed our first meeting with their parents—upper middle class, successful, business, professional, and academic people—and had had some interesting reactions that they might be willing to talk about. Soon the students came into the room, and sat at their desks in a circle. From the first I sensed something strange and wrong about the situation. There seemed a barrier between us. A week before they had been friendly and open; now most of them would hardly look at me. I felt a stranger and outsider. The teacher suggested that they might talk about their discussions with their parents, but though nobody refused, argued, or commented, it was clear after a minute or two that they did not want to and were not going to do that. So I tried to change the subject in a more general direction, toward the things we had talked about the week before. These the students were willing to talk about, but so differently from the way they had in our first meeting that I scarcely knew them for the same people. Before, their talk had been open, vigorous, natural, easy. Now it was full of the awkward, nervous, embarrassed, self-deprecatory phrases and gestures and giggles that we so often associate with teen-agers. I waited hopefully for this to change; it never did. One by one, in different ways, they told me the same story. They were no good. If they were not made to do things by older people, they would never do anything. The only things they really cared about were silly, trivial, and worthless, if not actually harmful. They were incompetent; they couldn't do anything; it was ridiculous to think of their being able to build a common room by themselves. Their only chance of doing anything or getting on in the world was to spend a great many more years doing exactly what the adults told them. Then, maybe, someday, they might amount to something. Maybe. They didn't even sound very sure about that. The hour crawled to its end. When the time was up, the students looked relieved. The teacher said that they all thanked me for coming to talk with them, but it was clear she spoke for herself. No student thanked me. None suggested in any way that they might want to talk about these things further, or indeed see me again. I wished them all good luck and left, with a heart of lead.

In many schools the problem is not that the students seem not to be interested in anything, or in only one thing, or that we can't find out what they're interested in. They are interested in many things, and once they trust us, and believe that we respect their interests, they will tell us, or show us what they are. The problem is that because of pressure from anxious or angry adults in the community, or our own worries about what is important, we are afraid to let the students think, talk, read, and write about what we know very well they are interested in. There have been and will be many conflicts over this. In many schools, all over the country, students have asked for and have been given, sometimes gladly, sometimes grudgingly, a day or several days, during which they can make their own program, have classes or seminars in what interests them, invite outside speakers and resource people and so on. In one school I know of, Shortridge High School in Indianapolis, the program lasted for an entire week—called Soul Week. The students put a great deal of work into it. They polled the entire student body to find out what subjects and seminars and activities people wanted to take part in, collated these, listed the activities for which there was the greatest demand, found resource people, made up a schedule, and went ahead. The program seemed a great success and involved many students. Some of the most popular courses and activities the school continued as part of the regular school curriculum. But in many communities in which the students have planned school programs, these have aroused a good deal of opposition in the community. Radical ideas! Frills! Why are they fooling around with this stuff instead of studying their school subjects?

One teacher, hearing this, said to me, "But I asked my students what they were interested in, and they wouldn't tell me, they just said, 'Nothing.'" I asked her if she had friends. Yes, she had. I asked if she knew something about their interests. Yes, she did. I said, "Did you find out by asking them 'What are your interests?'" She laughed. I said, "No, of course not. That's not how we find out. We find out by living with people, talking to them, getting to know them, seeing what they get excited about. It takes time and trust." In one of my fifth-grade classes, I discovered that one of the girls was not only crazy about horses, like almost all fifth-grade girls, but that she was an expert rider and jumper. From this I got the idea that she might like to read *National Velvet*, as in fact she did. From another boy I learned, a little bit from his conversation with other kids, a little from what he told me, mostly from what he was willing to write on his free papers, when he could stop worrying about spelling, punctuation, etc., that he was passionately interested in the woods, wild country, climbing, skiing, camping. All his writing was about travelers in a rugged country with night coming on, no shelter around, snow beginning to fall. From such clues I got the idea that he might like some of the books of Jack London (of whom he had never heard), and he did. And so for the others in the class. But I never would have learned these things in a conventional class, no matter what sort of questions I might have asked. I had to try to create an atmosphere in which the children, free to be themselves, would show their interests, let them come out. Then and only then was I able to help them go further with what they already liked.

It is easy to talk about legitimizing the interests of students and getting into honest communication with them. But there are still more than a few schools in which a teacher who tries to do this may meet increasing opposition, may be ordered to stop, and if he persists may be fired. How much this is so has much to do with the social and economic class of the students. In a school where most of the students go to college, there is a general feeling that words and ideas are important, even if they are only the words and ideas that belong to the school. The school knows that it will be judged by how its students do in the word and idea oriented worlds of college, graduate school, and professional life. Any one in such a school who tries to get the students talking and thinking has at least a chance of getting a sympathetic hearing—though as many teachers have already found out, this is by no means certain. In a lower-income school, the situation may be tougher. Nobody there expects most of the children to go to college. When they get out of school, they are going to have to start doing dull and pointless work, and they will be doing it for the rest of their lives. To the parents and teachers of such students, words, thoughts, ideas are dangerous. They say, "Don't give these kids (my kids) ideas; they'll just get them in trouble. Teach them to keep their mouths shut, their noses clean, and to do what they're told. That way they'll get along fine."

A teacher in such a school who tries to legitimize the interests of his students, take them seriously, talk to them honestly, and give them some sense of worth and self-respect may well be seen, by fellow teachers, administration, and parents as an intolerable threat. This is not a guess; it has happened many times. Word of what he is doing will seep out. The students will look, feel, and talk differently. They may begin to stand up for their rights, against the kind of official bullies and petty tyrants shown in the film *High School*. Or they may just begin to stand up. One of the things that saddens me most in many high schools is the hangdog look on the faces of so many of the students. This look is not an accident. The schools, and often the parents, have worked hard to put it there, and they will be alarmed and angry if they begin not to see it. Many schools expect their students to look servile, and if they start looking otherwise, will look for the cause and will trace it to the teacher. The teacher himself will begin to have a relationship with the students quite different from that of the other adults in the school. This too will be noticed and opposed. Finally, as the teacher knows the students better and begins to make human connections with them, he may not be able, even if he wants to, to avoid being drawn more and more into their struggles with the arbitrariness and injustice of the school. He will begin to take their side. This may well be the last straw.

There is no easy remedy for this. Teachers who want to work in an open and humane way with lower-income high school students would do well to find a school in which they are already treated fairly and humanely, or at least a school in which the administration would like to move in this direction. Some radical student teachers seem to feel that their duty is to find an authoritarian and rigid school and, by teaching in it and struggling with it, to try to make it more humane. I think the task may well be impossible, and that they will just get themselves fired. This may be a very useful experience for them, but the school will go on much as it is. In short, an oppressive high school in a low-income community may not be a very promising place for a teacher to work in to bring about educational change.

HERBERT KOHL
Beginning the School Year

Expectations

Teachers begin the school year burdened with expectations and preconceptions that often interfere with the development of open classrooms. Classes are "tracked" and students are placed together according to academic achievement. Reading achievement or I.Q. scores are usually used to decide which track a student "belongs" in, though sometimes teachers' judgments about their students' potential count too. There are top, middle, and bottom classes; A, B, C, and D "streams." No matter how schools try to conceal this grouping, the pupils know where they are placed. Bottom classes, the C and D streams, often tell their teachers at the beginning of the school year, "You can't expect much from us. We're dumb."

Teachers know the type of class they are expected to be teaching.[1] Before the teacher has even met his students his expectations of bright, mediocre, or dull individuals are set.

Even in schools which have abandoned tracking, the teacher is given a set of record cards by his supervisor which document the child's school life as perceived by his previous teachers. These cards usually contain achievement and I.Q. scores, personality evaluations, descriptions of conferences with the students' parents, judgments about his behavior in class and "study habits." Difficult pupils are identified as well as good

---

"Beginning the School Year" by Herbert Kohl. Reprinted with permission from *The New York Review of Books.* Copyright © 1969 by Herbert Kohl.

[1] In some Union contracts there are even provisions for rotation of teachers from top to bottom, through the middle to the top again.

(i.e., conforming and performing) ones. The record cards are probably designed not only as analyses of their pupils' careers at school, but as warnings to teachers on what to expect.

When the teacher meets his class on the first day of the school year, he is armed with all of this "professional" knowledge. Anticipating a dull class, for example, a teacher may have spent several weeks preparing simple exercises to keep his students busy. On the other hand, faced with the prospect of teaching a bright class, he may have found a new and challenging textbook or devised some ingenious scientific experiments.

If the record cards indicate that several pupils are particularly troublesome or, what is more threatening, "disturbed," the teacher will single them out as soon as they enter the room and treat them differently from the other pupils. He may do the same with bright students or ones rumored to be wise, funny, lazy, violent, scheming, deceitful. . . . The students will sense this and act in the manner expected of them. Thus the teacher traps both himself and his pupils into repeating patterns that have been set for years.

Expectations influence behavior in subtle ways: a successful though nervous and unhappy student may try to relax. His teacher says, "What's the matter? You're not yourself this week." This may produce feelings of guilt in the student, who then drives himself to succeed in spite of feeling that the price he is paying for academic achievement may be excessive.

A "difficult" student tries to make a new start and is quiet and obedient. His teacher responds to this behavior by saying, "You're off to a good start this year," and so informs the student that a bad start was expected of him. The student becomes angry and defiant.

A supposedly dull student gives a correct answer in class and is praised excessively. He is embarrassed and becomes withdrawn.

Even in kindergarten a teacher will have expectations. Some children are "disadvantaged," others have language problems. The teacher anticipates that they may not do well. Others come from intellectual or privileged homes and if they don't perform well something must be wrong.

Teachers' expectations have a tendency to become self-fulfilling.[2] "Bad" classes tend to act badly, and "gifted" classes tend to respond to the special consideration that they expect to be given to them if they perform in a "superior" way.

All of this is inimical to an open classroom, where the role of the teacher is not to control his pupils but rather to enable them to make

[2] For a study of self-fulfilling prophesies, see *Pygmalion in the Classroom: Teacher Expectation and the Pupil's Intellectual Ability*, by Robert Rosenthal and Lenore Jacobson, Holt, Rinehart & Winston, 1968, $4.95; $3.95 (paper).

choices and pursue what interests them. In an open classroom a pupil functions according to his sense of himself rather than what he is expected to be. It is not that the teacher should expect the same of all his pupils. On the contrary, the teacher must learn to perceive differences, but these should emerge from what actually happens in the classroom during the school year, and not from preconceptions.

I remember an incident where the effect of a teacher's expectations in one of my classes was pernicious. I have always been unable to avoid having favorites in my classes. I like defiant, independent, and humorous people, and my preferences naturally come out in my teaching. One year, several students were puzzled by my choice of favorites. The class had been together for three years and each year teachers chose the same four children as their favorite students. However, I had chosen different students and it upset most of the class, especially the ones who had been favorites in the past. All the students were black. It took me several months to realize that the former favorites were all the lightest-skinned pupils in the class—in other words, the whitest were (by their white teachers) expected to be the nicest and most intelligent.

A teacher in an open classroom needs to cultivate a state of *suspended expectations*. It is not easy. It is easy to believe that a dull class is dull, or a bright class is bright. The words "emotionally disturbed" conjure up frightening images. And it is sometimes a relief to discover that there are good pupils in the class that is waiting for you. Not reading the record cards or ignoring the standing of the class is an act of self-denial: it involves casting aside a crutch when one still believes one can't walk without it. Yet if one wants to develop an open classroom within the context of a school which is essentially totalitarian, such acts of will are necessary.

What does it mean to suspend expectations when one is told that the class one will be teaching is slow, or bright, or ordinary? At the least it means not preparing to teach in any special way or deciding beforehand on the complexity of the materials to be used during a school year. It means that planning does not consist of finding the class's achievement level according to the record cards and tailoring the material to those levels, but rather preparing diverse materials and subjects and discovering from the students as the year unfolds what is relevant to them and what isn't.

Particularly it means not reading I.Q. scores or achievement scores, not discovering who may be a source of trouble and who a solace or even a joy. It means giving your pupils a fresh chance to develop in new ways in your classroom, freed from the roles they may have adopted during their previous school careers. It means allowing children to become who they care to become, and freeing the teacher from the standards by which new pupils had been measured in the past.

There are no simple ways to give up deeply rooted expectations. There are some suggestions, however:

—talk to students outside class
—watch them play and watch them live with other young people
—play with them—joking games and serious games
—talk to them about yourself, what you care about
—listen

In these situations the kids may surprise you and reveal rather than conceal, as is usual in the classroom, their feelings, playfulness, and intelligence.

The First Day of School

The students walk into the room the teacher has been assigned. The school year has begun. Usually the class sits down before the teacher makes his first remarks. Sometimes the class stands up, waiting. Whatever happens, the first move of the school year is the teacher's.

He introduces himself, calls the roll of pupils' names (usually in alphabetical order), and then assigns seats.

The assignment of seats, perhaps the first act the teacher performs during the school year, can stand symbolically for many things that occur in authoritarian classrooms. It is the teacher who assigns the seats and the pupils who must obey. Even in those few classes where the pupils are allowed to choose their seats it is usually made clear that once chosen, the seats can't be changed.

Usually the order of seating is quite arbitrary according to the size and sex of pupils or by alphabetical order. The primary function of this order seems to be to provide the teacher with an immediate way of knowing where his pupils are so they can't put anything over on him before he learns their names. During the course of the year the teacher adjusts the seating according to his convenience or need, isolating troublemakers, rewarding good pupils, etc. But it is always the teacher who commands.

An open classroom is different. Pupils are free to choose and change their seats. So is the teacher. When disputes arise they must be adjudicated and finally settled with all parties involved. If two people want the same seat they must settle it with each other and with the teacher and with other pupils. There is, of course, no formula for resolving all conflicts. It is a matter of learning how to bargain and compromise. But one must make sure that an authoritarian structure controlled by pupils does not replace the one the teacher has refused to impose. This is a difficult and delicate matter.

Young people in American schools are used to authoritarian methods. They experience them in school, in their families, and in society at large. They cannot be expected to fit into a more open situation without misgivings and without, in some circumstances, assuming the authoritarian roles their teachers have abdicated. They are used to controlling or being controlled and will often be harder on each other than are the most oppressive adults.

Children playing school can be incredibly cruel. I remember watching a group of nine- and ten-year-old girls playing school. The "teacher" had a stick and she was whacking the other girls, screaming at them, forcing them to spell words out loud, and berating them for always being wrong. It took me quite a while to realize that correct spelling was irrelevant to the game since neither the "teacher" nor her "pupils" knew or cared about the correct spelling of words. They were acting out the role of the omniscient teacher and the ignorant pupil. For them being a teacher meant exercising control and being a pupil meant being submissive.

Yet a classroom can become more democratic. People can come to listen to each other and care about each other's thoughts and feelings. It takes patience, and a belief in the potential of the children. Time must be taken, especially in the beginning of the school year, to work out disputes over seating and other seemingly petty things like hanging up coats, lining up, and going in and out of the school building. When these are done without specific directions and without imposing sanctions against offenders, some disputes are bound to arise. That is the price of developing a democratic classroom where pupils and teacher find ways of functioning together without invoking arbitrary or absolute authority.

I have seen the most defeated students, the ones most thoroughly oppressed in school, coming back year after year, looking fresh and open on the first day of school, ready to put their failure and despair and cynicism aside and begin again, if only it were made possible for them to do so.

Rules and Routines

It is difficult for beginning teachers to establish control because they have not yet sensed that control comes as much through imposing rules and routines as it does from the personal authority of the teacher. Not having had a class of their own yet, they can't imagine the degree to which routine (and not curriculum, not learning, not teaching) can be used to control and contain the behavior of students. When my wife first taught, she was overwhelmed by the number of things she had to do that seemed to have nothing to do with teaching. She had to call the roll; line up her pupils; organize fire drills; pass out and collect papers, books, and pencils; lead the pledge to the flag; collect milk and lunch money, and so on. Failing to perceive how these extraneous activities contributed to maintaining control in the classroom, she was exasperated. A second-year teacher, sensing her frustration, reassured her that after the first year it wasn't so bad. "In fact," she said, "after the first year teaching is just like being a secretary." Once you get your routines straight you can control space and time in your environment. The content or quality of what you are doing is irrelevant.

It is not only routines and rules that shore up the authoritarian classroom. Textbooks and workbooks have the same function. The first year it may be difficult to get the knack of using them, but after that one can do the same thing year after year—read the same stories, ask the same questions, get the same answers. It may get boring but it also gets easier. Chance occurrences are minimized.

In an open classroom it is different. Each school year is unique for both the students and the teacher. The first day is not filled with the mastery of routines and the pronouncement of rules. It is not possible to anticipate which rules or routines will emerge as convenient or necessary for a particular class. Nor is it desirable to announce rigid rules and routines when they may prove irrelevant or cumbersome later in the year, and one may want to abandon them. Just as one has to suspend expectations with respect to individual students, so with respect to rules and routines one must suspend one's fear of chaos.

One must face one's fear that young people will run wild if they are not held down or controlled. The spectre of chaos haunts many teachers, probably because they don't believe in their own strength or ability to handle the power they assume. Yet there is no need to impose rules or pull rank. It is possible to assume that rules and routines are necessary only as they emerge as indispensable for the group's functioning. If students find ways to line up and sit down, hang up their coats, choose and change their seats with a minimum of problems, why bother to restrict them by rigid routines? If discussion can develop without the students raising their hands, why bother with that procedure? As teachers are more willing to take chances with new ways of acting they may find it increasingly possible to be themselves and relax with young people.

However, hanging up coats in the morning, for example, may become a real problem if students fight over hooks or take things from each other's pockets or throw coats on the floor. In these circumstances something must be done—the problem can't be ignored without destroying respect for the teacher as an honest and strong person. But that does not mean that the teacher should legislate the problem of coats out of existence. The people in the class must deal with it as their problem and come to some resolution.

The students involved can, for example, settle the matter in private with the teacher adjudicating. The problem can also be settled by the class in a general discussion or a mock trial. There are theatrical and playful ways to deal with the problem of coathooks too. The teacher can suggest that the whole class try to hang their coats on one hook, or do without hooks for a day, or find other places in the classroom to store their coats. Then the question of storing coats can be discussed in a general way or in relationship to the coat games. The initial incident can be forgotten or made to seem insignificant.

All this may take time—time that will be taken away from reading and science and social studies and other supposedly basic work. One must learn to respond to what happens spontaneously in the classroom and to put aside one's other plans. This is as true with matters of curriculum as with "discipline" problems. For example, a short story may refer to an earthquake in passing and the class may be more interested in discussing earthquakes than in finishing the story. Or in studying motion in physics some students may want to look into motion in dance or track. A math lesson on probability theory can lead to a crap game and even to a historical study of the origins of dice. A discussion of the French Revolution can lead by association to a study of instruments of execution, of penal institutions, and finally the role of law in an unjust society. A teacher has to learn to go with the class, to respond to their desire to learn about things and not cut off their enthusiasm in the service of getting through the curriculum. It is necessary to take time to solve problems communally. The democratic development of routines and rules and restrictions is as crucial to the development of freedom in an open classroom as the arbitrary imposition of them is central to control in an authoritarian class.

The concept of order in an open classroom is not the same as that current in the schools where rules and routines are developed to avoid disagreements. In most classrooms there is no place for argument or conflict, nor is there time for teachers and pupils to learn how to live with and listen to each other. There is no give-and-take. The students direct their talk to the teacher, and obey the teacher's rules. Conflict, defiance, or disagreement are disciplinary problems and offenders must be punished. In an open classroom there is considerable give-and-take, argument, disagreement, even conflict. These are organic elements in the life of the group, to be dealt with and resolved by the group and arbitrated by the teacher. The teacher is a mediator and not a judge or executioner.

Students may have disputes about where they want to sit, or how to line up. It may take a while for them to learn to talk or listen to each other or to the teacher. But in the classroom—as in life—it is more dangerous to legislate disagreement out of existence than to accept and integrate it into the whole.

The first day of school does not have to consist of proclaiming rules and practicing routines. There are other things a teacher can do on the first day. It depends upon his style and personality, the subject he is teaching, the age of the students—any number of things. The important point, however, is that in an open classroom the teacher is no more required to behave like a "teacher" than the students are required to be submissive children. The teacher needn't always be at the front of the room and lead, nor does he have to speak "proper" English, nor defend a rigid system of "right" and "wrong." He can be in the classroom the same complex person he is in life and relieve himself of the strain of assuming what he thinks to be the appropriate persona. He needn't be afraid of the students learning his first name, nor of talking with the class about his "private" life and experiences, his confusions, defeats, and triumphs. He can use his own experiences to help his students deal with theirs.

Often on the first day students are asked to write an essay on themselves, or a theme on "what I did last summer." Such assignments may be well intentioned, but they miss something crucial. The students are asked to write about themselves and their experiences. What about the teacher? Shouldn't the students have as much opportunity to assess the teacher's words as he theirs? One way of beginning a school year is by telling the pupils about yourself—where you came from, where you are, and where you think you are going. Then it may make more sense to the students to talk of themselves in reasonably open and honest ways.

Another thing that can be done the first day is to introduce the students to the room you will share with them for the year. Show them the furniture and books in the room and tell them of other resources available. Show them the supplies and equipment in the room, open the doors to them. Ask students what they would like to do with what is available. Suggest that they add to the richness of the environment by bringing in things they care about. Talk about what you are interested in doing yourself. There is no need to preach a nonauthoritarian sermon and many reasons for not doing it. Students generally distrust all sermons, regardless of their message. An open classroom develops through the actions of the teacher and not because of his words.

An Ordinary Classroom and a Not So Ordinary One

Teachers must learn to work in open and creative ways themselves if they want their classrooms to become less authoritarian. Recently I conducted a seminar for teachers which was designed to get the participants to do things rather than to talk about techniques of teaching.

For example, instead of discussing the teaching of writing or music or painting, we wrote, made music, and painted.

During one session we all tried to think back to our own earliest experiences in school and to recreate them in writing or through drawing. Most of our memories went back to kindergarten or the first grade, and an unusual number of them were spatial. I remembered my first-grade classroom and how confined and boxlike it felt. The tables were placed in rows and their tops were hard and rectangular. I was afraid that I would move things from their proper places and walked cautiously whenever I left my seat. For the most part I tried to disappear into my chair, hide from the teacher, and let my imagination invest the room with wild and secret places.

Many of the other teachers had similar memories. Some remembered windows they were not allowed to look out of, books and papers that had to be treated reverently, chalk boards with rules and assignments posted on them, new briefcases that had to be kept neat and clean. The drawings were full of boxes representing rooms, papers, books, tables, buildings; our memories of school were predominantly closed and rectangular.

It is no accident that spatial memories are strong. The placement of objects in space is not arbitrary and rooms represent in physical form the spirit and souls of places and institutions. A teacher's room tells us something about how he is and a great deal about what he is doing.

Often we are not aware of the degree to which the spaces we control give us away, nor conscious of how much we could learn of ourselves by looking at the spaces we live in. It is important for teachers to look at the spatial dimensions of their classrooms, to step back so they may see how the organization of space represents the life lived within it. To illustrate this and give a picture of what differences exist from classroom to classroom I would like to consider some hypothetical classrooms, each with identical furniture and dimensions yet arranged by different teachers. I'll start by examining the spatial organization of these rooms on the first day of school, and then look back at them during the middle of the school year. In this way it may be possible to show the many seemingly minor yet crucial ways in which an open classroom differs from an authoritarian and closed one.

The rooms I have in mind can be found in most schools in the United States. They are rectangular in shape, not too large, and contain chalk boards, bulletin boards, cabinets, windows, and perhaps closets, arranged around the periphery of the rectangle. Occasionally there are a sink and drinking fountain and, in exceptional cases, toilets built into the room. The interior has no partitions and is occupied by combinations of chairs, desks, desk chairs, and tables. The desks are rectangular and the tables rectangular or round. Sometimes the chairs and desks are bolted to the floor but there is a tendency to have movable furniture in newer buildings. The teacher's desk is distinguished from the pupils' desks by its size and the presence of abundant drawer space.[3]

There are some classrooms which also have bookcases, magazine racks, work benches, and easels. Also there are usually wastebaskets in the room.

These are the common elements—now let's turn to the way they are fitted into the classroom environments. The first teacher[4] I want to consider has had several years' experience; she is talented and popular with her pupils. In her room the authoritarian mode of teaching does not seem particularly oppressive. She is an attractive woman and spends time trying to make her room as pleasant as possible. This fits very well with her teaching style. She is quite friendly with her students in a maternal way and prides herself on being able to get them to perform well. She enjoys teaching gifted children the most, but will take her turn with the less bright classes. She is a bit of a cynic yet gets along with the staff. Her main fault (though it is not seen as such by her coworkers) is a deep intolerance of, and dislike for, defiant and "lazy" pupils.

This teacher works very hard getting her classroom in order before the first day of class. She has read the class record cards, knows how many girls and boys there are, who the troublemakers are likely to be. She arranges the desks, tables, and chairs accordingly. The wall with the chalk board is designated the front of the room (many teachers don't realize that this needn't be the case), making the opposite wall the back of the room, and the two remaining walls the sides. This may seem a simpleminded thing to mention but it isn't. Why does a classroom have to have to have a front, a back and two sides? The notion that there is a "front of the class" and the authoritarian mode of delivering knowledge received from above to students who are below—both go together.

Having designated the front of the room, the teacher moves all the tables and desks into a position where they face the chalk board. They are also arranged in evenly spaced rows. Chairs are placed accordingly, one to a desk, or to a designated place around a table. Extra chairs and tables are set aside until the teacher's desk is in place. The teacher I'm describing is sympathetic to the progressive movement in education. She doesn't believe that the teacher should put her desk in the front of the room, even though she accepts the notion of a "front" of the room. Consequently she moves her desk to the side, a bit apart from the students' desks but in a convenient position to survey them.

An extra table, round if possible, is placed in the back of the room. The wastebasket is placed next to the teacher's desk.

---

[3] In colleges teachers are often given lecterns or their desks are placed on platforms or above the level of their students' chairs.

[4] These portraits are fictional versions of classrooms I've visited.

So much for the movable furniture. Next the teacher turns to the chalk board. On the far right (or left) of the chalk board in the front of the room the teacher prints neatly her name (prefaced by Miss), the class designation, room number, and several other things that may look like this:

>Miss A. Levinton
>Class 6-543 (hs)
>Date
>Attendance: B_____ G_____
>Assignment:
>Homework:

After the chalk board come the bulletin boards. The teacher has prepared ingenious and elegant displays to put up around the room. There are photographs, charts, signs, maps—things designed to illustrate and illuminate the curriculum for the year and make the classroom handsome though somewhat antiseptic. A small part of one bulletin board is set aside and neatly labeled "Students' Work."

The bookcase in the back of the room holds the books the teacher has accumulated, and the table in the back of the room is labeled "Library Corner." The cabinets and closets are full of neatly stacked books and papers and the teacher checks to see that their doors are all closed. Another closet, one with a lock, has been set aside as the teacher's closet. It has been stocked with a smock, some comfortable shoes, a coffee cup and saucer, and a bottle of instant coffee, etc. It also contains a metal box with the students' record cards.

The class room is ready to receive its students. The teacher has made the room a familiar place for her to function in and, armed with rules and routines, is ready to face her new class and tell them exactly what will be expected of them in the coming year. The students are free to fit in or be thrown out.

A visitor to the class three months later would be struck by the similarities of the room on the first day and ninety days later. A few changes would be evident, however. There would be neat papers on the bulletin board under the label "Students' Work," as well as a new but equally elegant bulletin board display. There would also be books and papers in the students' desks. But the wastebasket would still be next to the teacher's desk and the library would still be bare except for its label. All would be in order.

It is hard to distinguish between apparent chaos and creative disorder. The next classroom I will describe could present problems for an observer; he would have to attend as much to what is not done as to what is done. Interesting and natural patterns of classroom life can emerge through a collaboration of all the people involved; but this may take time and patience, and one has to have seen the process of development in order to understand the result.

When the second teacher I have in mind arrives before the start of school, the classroom is a mess. The chairs have been piled upon the tables and pushed into a corner. The teacher, a young man who has taught for several years, can't make up his mind what to do with the furniture. As he enters his room he feels disoriented. He can't tell the front of the room from the rear. It strikes him that there may be advantages in seeing the room as a neutral space without points of orientation. Perhaps his students would also be struck by the neutrality of the space and see for the first time that many things could be done with it.

Why not leave the room just as it is and see what happens when the students enter? He had other plans, ones carefully nurtured over the summer. He would set up the tables in small groups and let the children sit where they chose. He would also turn the teacher's desk into a resource table which he would occupy at certain times and which could, he hoped, become the communications center of the classroom rather than the seat of power and authority. But the idea of leaving things as they are may be a better way to begin the year. Perhaps it might be possible to make organization of the class a collaborative venture between him and his students, and among the students themselves. Besides, he has come to realize that the things that work best in class for him are the unplanned ones, the ones that arise spontaneously because of a student's suggestion or a sudden perception. He trusts his intuitions and isn't too upset to abandon plans that had consumed time and energy.

The previous year he had run a reasonably open classroom. Still he had organized the room from front to back; and though the tables and chairs were movable, they faced in only one direction during the year. He had used the class record cards to tell him who his pupils were though he very frequently found them misleading and inaccurate. For half the year he'd used textbooks and finally got up the courage to drop them after one of his pupils turned in a devastating parody of one of the stories in the book. He had worried that the principal of the school might object to this but he did not announce what he was doing and no one complained. During the remainder of the year he built a library of students' writing and books to replace the textbooks. He found one interesting set of readers and kept them because he liked group reading himself and wanted to have one book he could read together with his students and discuss with them. That was one of his pleasures in teaching.

He also managed to piece together a set of dictionaries and obtain a record player and a collection of records, a slide machine, a $15 tape recorder, tapes and film strips, and a miscellaneous collection of junk that filled the closets of the room leaving him no place to hang his coat. He took to hanging it in the wardrobe along with his students' coats.

The stuff he had collected the previous year was still in the closets and cabinets. He threw open all the doors in the room as he had planned. The blackboard and bulletin boards in the room had been untouched since June as he had requested. Except for the tables and chairs everything was as it was the last day of school the previous year.

The plan was quite simple. The first day of school would consist of a dismantling of the previous year's work, an examination of things in the classroom by the new students, and an exploration of what was available. He didn't want to impose a structure upon the class; at the same time he knew that it was crucial to have enough stuff in his room to suggest to his pupils the range of things they might do.

It is impossible to predict what his classroom would look like after three months. That would depend upon the students and the teacher, and also upon what happened to be engaging their attention at the moment. Things would most certainly be in a state of flux. Certain groupings of chairs and tables would be just forming, others would be in the process of distintegration. The bulletin boards would be full of the students' works, or of pictures they liked or the teacher liked. Some might look worn but sacred and bound to last out the year; others would be in the process of being assembled or dismantled. The stuff—the record player, tape recorder, books, etc.—would be distributed throughout the room and there is no telling where the wastebasket would be. Those who need it would use it—and would not have to come up to the teacher's desk in order to throw things out.

The teacher's desk might also be anywhere. It might not even be the teacher's any more, the teacher settling for a desk like the pupils' and abandoning his privileged piece of furniture to some other use.

In order to find out what this all meant, an observer would have to discover what the pupils were doing and what the teacher was doing at that particular moment in the year. The observer might not discover chaos, however, but a more complex and freer order than is usually found in classrooms in the United States, or in the society at large for that matter.

PUBLIC SCHOOLS: BEYOND PEDAGOGY

The last two essays included here, like those in the preceding section, are ostensibly about the classroom. But in actuality they take us in another direction entirely, out of the classroom and back into the world. For both Jim Herndon and Sylvia Ashton-Warner, even the limits of the open classroom are too self-consciously "educational" to be taken seriously. Their concern is with experience rather than education, with the world rather than the classroom, and that shift of attention and focus takes us back, full circle, to where this collection began: to the limits of schooling. Once again, as with de-schooling or some free-schooling, one finds a rejection of pedagogic terms and concerns and an insistent reliance on the natural shapes and motions of the larger world. But where writers like Neill or Goodman take us out of the schools in order to escape them, both Herndon and Warner try to destroy those limits while remaining in the schools. They allow into the classroom the full world of experience so that the young can inhabit it, so that it can destroy, as it does, all previous conceptions about learning, schooling or teaching.

It is no accident that both Herndon and Ashton-Warner, like Paul Goodman, are novelists as well as teachers, more concerned with protecting and honoring experience than in changing it. Their attitudes toward the classroom are close to the modern writer's or painter's attitude toward a work; precisely the same revolution in form that occurred in the arts occurs in their classrooms. The form itself is broken—

not in order to "improve" things, but merely to allow back into it the turbulence and depth of life that had previously been excluded, for without that turbulence and depth there is no meaning to form. For Herndon, what has been excluded and must now be readmitted is simply the domestic truth of day-to-day reality, the low-humming, unmanaged life of the world which makes its way into the classroom in the eccentric natures of his students. For Ashton-Warner, it is the life of the imagination, the ways in which the unseen possibilities of expression reside in each student, waiting to be allowed in. For her, as with Herndon, the proper relation to the excluded world is less a question of technique than of attitude; it is a question of *reception*: the willingness to make room in the world, even in schools, for what it is one genuinely loves.

That genuine love, a passion for life, takes us past the idea of "helping" or "teaching" and into a new realm altogether, one in which even such well-meant devices as the open classroom are left behind. Of course there is nothing here which would be alien or distressing to someone like John Holt or Herb Kohl, and yet it all takes us one step past them, for there is a freedom of activity here and a passion for unmanaged activity never fully expressed in what they write. That may be, of course, because both Holt and Kohl address themselves to teachers, to the timidity and caution of teachers, and so they speak *sotto voce*, using, still, the language of pedagogy. But here that language gives way to the language of experience, and there is something restorative in that, for it takes us a bit closer to our true size and depth; we leave behind the incessant desire to control and improve things, and begin, instead, to honor and inhabit them.

Herndon's first book was called *The Way It Spozed To Be*, and the title was taken from the complaints his students always nervously made when he did things out of the ordinary: *but that ain't the way it spozed to be*. What Herndon and Ashton-Warner both know is that the way it isn't spozed to be is the way that it actually *is*. There is no right or wrong way, no methodological answer to things, not even in the open classroom; there is simply life itself, the changing shapes of the world in and around us, and the ways in which, in the midst of them, we accept and summon forth the possibilities of experience. The central problem is not how to correct or control those possibilities, but simply to somehow keep them whole in the face of everything designed to destroy them. Though that may not seem like much at first, it may be more important than any kind of technique, may demand more from a teacher than any change in methodology. For what such activity demands is nothing less than an ability to love the world, a willingness to honor its variety above all intentionality and schooling. That may not, in itself, be enough to change things; in the end, no doubt, it must be coupled, for the sake of wholeness, with the kinds of larger vision and political concern to be found in Illich or Goodman. But that larger vision remains pointless and empty of meaning unless there is kept at its center the love of life one finds in Herndon or Ashton-Warner. Without that we forget who we are, what we ought to be, or why we bother with any of this in the first place.

SYLVIA ASHTON-WARNER

The Unlived Life

It's all so merciful on a teacher, this appearance of the subjects of an infant room in the creative vent. For one thing, the drive is no longer the teacher's but the children's own. And for another, the teacher is at last with the stream and not against it: the stream of children's inexorable creativeness. As Dr. Jung says, psychic life is a world power that exceeds by many times all the powers of the earth; as Dr. Burrow says, the secret of our collective ills is to be traced to the suppression of creative ability; and as Erich Fromm says, destructiveness is the outcome of the unlived life.

So it is of more than professional moment that all of the work of young children should be through the creative vent. It is more than a teaching matter or a dominion one. It's an international matter. So often I have said in the past, when a war is over the statesmen should not go into conference with one another but should turn their attention to the infant rooms, since it is from there that comes peace or war. And that's how I see organic teaching. It helps to set the creative pattern in a mind while it is yet malleable, and in this role is a humble contribution to peace.

The expansion of a child's mind can be a beautiful growth. And in beauty are included the qualities of equilibrium, harmony and rest. There's no more comely word in the language than "rest." All the movement in life, and out of it too, is towards a condition of rest. Even the simple movement of a child "coming up."

From *Teacher* by Sylvia Ashton-Warner. Copyright © 1963 by Sylvia Ashton-Warner. Reprinted by permission of Simon & Schuster, Inc.

I can't disassociate the activity in an infant room from peace and war. So often I have seen the destructive vent, beneath an onslaught of creativity, dry up under my eyes. Especially with the warlike Maori five-year-olds who pass through my hands in hundreds, arriving with no other thought in their heads other than to take, break, fight and be first. With no opportunity for creativity they may well develop, as they did in the past, with fighting as their ideal of life. Yet all this can be expelled through the creative vent, and the more violent the boy the more I see that he creates, and when he kicks the others with his big boots, treads on fingers on the mat, hits another over the head with a piece of wood or throws a stone, I put clay in his hands, or chalk. He can create bombs if he likes or draw my house in flame, but it is the creative vent that is widening all the time and the destructive one atrophying, however much it may look to the contrary. And anyway I have always been more afraid of the weapon unspoken than of the one on a blackboard.

With all this in mind therefore I try to bring as many facets of teaching into the creative vent as possible, with emphasis on reading and writing. And that's just what organic teaching is; all subjects in the creative vent. It's just as easy for a teacher, who gives a child a brush and lets him paint, to give him a pencil and let him write, and to let him pass his story to the next one to read. Simplicity is so safe. There's no occasion whatever for the early imposition of a dead reading, a dead vocabulary. I'm so afraid of it. It's like a frame over a young tree making it grow in an unnatural shape. It makes me think of that curtailment of a child's expansion of which Erich Fromm speaks, of that unlived life of which destructiveness is the outcome. "And instead of the wholeness of the expansive tree we have only the twisted and stunted bush." The trouble is that a child from a modern respectable home suffers such a serious frame on his behaviour long before he comes near a teacher. Nevertheless I think that after a year of organic work the static vocabularies can be used without misfortune. They can even, under the heads of external stimulus and respect for the standard of English, become desirable.

But only when built upon the organic foundation. And there's hardly anything new in the conception of progress from the known to the unknown. It's just that when the inorganic reading is imposed first it interferes with integration; and it's upon the integrated personality that everything is built. We've lost the gracious movement from the inside outward. We overlook the footing. I talk sometimes about a bridge from the pa to the European environment, but there is a common bridge for a child of any race and of more moment than any other: the bridge from the inner world outward. And that is what organic teaching is. An indispensable step in integration. Without it we get this one-patterned mind of the New Zealand child, accruing from so much American influence of the mass-mind type. I think that we already have so much pressure towards sameness through radio, film and comic outside the school, that we can't afford to do a thing inside that is not toward individual development, and from this stance I can't see that we can indulge in the one imposed reading for all until the particular variety of a mind is set. And a cross-section of children from different places in New Zealand provides me with an automatic check on the progress of the one-patterned mind. (I own seventy fancy-dress costumes which I lend.) All the children want the same costumes. If you made dozens of cowboy and cowgirl costumes, hundreds of Superman and thousands of Rocket Man costumes and hired them at half a guinea a go, you'd get every penny of it and would make a fortune vast enough to retire on and spend the rest of your life in the garden. As for my classics—Bo-Peep, the Chinese Mandarin, Peter Pan and the Witch and so on—they so gather the dust that they have had to be folded and put away. It's this sameness in children that can be so boring. So is death boring.

To write peaceful reading books and put them in an infant room is not the way to peace. They don't even scratch the surface. No child ever asked for a Janet or a John costume. There is only one answer to destructiveness and that is creativity. And it never was and never will be any different. And when I say so I am in august company.

The noticeable thing in New Zealand society is the body of people with their inner resources atrophied. Seldom have they had to reach inward to grasp the thing that they wanted. Everything, from material requirements to ideas, is available ready-made. From mechanical gadgets in the shops to sensation in the films they can buy almost anything they fancy. They can buy life itself from the film and radio—canned life.

And even if they tried to reach inward for something that maybe they couldn't find manufactured, they would no longer find anything there. They've dried up. From babyhood they have had shiny toys put in their hands, and in the kindergartens and infant rooms bright pictures and gay material. Why conceive anything of their own? There has not been the need. The capacity to do so has been atrophied and now there is nothing there. The vast expanses of the mind that could have been alive with creative activity are now no more than empty vaults that must, for comfort's sake, be filled with non-stop radio, and their conversation consists of a list of platitudes and clichés.

I can't quite understand why.

From what I see of modern education the intention is just the opposite: to let children grow up in their own personal way into creative and interesting people. Is it the standard textbooks? Is it the consolidation? Is it the quality of the teachers? Is it the access to film and radio and the quality of those luxuries? Or is it the access to low-grade reading material infused through all of these things? I don't know where the intention fails but we end up with the same pattern of a person in nine hundred ninety-nine instances out of a thousand.

I said to a friend of mine, a professor, recently, "What kind of children arrive at the University to you?" He said, "They're all exactly the same." "But," I said, "how can it be like that? The whole plan of primary education at least is for diversity." "Well," he answered, "they come to me like samples from a mill. Not one can think for himself. I beg them not to serve back to me exactly what I have given to them. I challenge them sometimes with wrong statements to provoke at least some disagreement but even that won't work." "But," I said, "you must confess to about three per cent originality." "One in a thousand," he replied. "One in a thousand."

On the five-year-old level the mind is not yet patterned and it is an exciting thought. True, I often get the over-disciplined European five, crushed beyond recognition as an identity, by respectable parents, but never Maoris; as a rule a five-year-old child is not boring. In an infant room it is still possible to meet an interesting, unpatterned person. "In the infant room," I told this professor, "we still have identity. It's somewhere between my infant-room level and your university level that the story breaks. But I don't think it is the plan of education itself."

I think that the educational story from the infant room to the university is like the writing of a novel. You can't be sure of your beginning until you have checked it with your ending. What might come of infant teachers visiting the university and professors visiting the infant room? I had two other professors in my infant room last year and they proved themselves to be not only delightfully in tune but sensitively helpful.

Yet what I believe and what I practise are not wholly the same thing. For instance, although I have reason to think that a child's occupation until seven should not be other than creative in the many mediums, nevertheless I find myself teaching some things.

With all this in mind, therefore, the intent of the infant room is the nurturing of the organic idea,

the preservation of the inner resources,
the exercise of the inner eye and
the protraction of the true personality.

I like unpredictability and variation; I like drama and I like gaiety; I like peace in the world and I like interesting people, and all this means that I like life in its organic shape and that's just what you get in an infant room where the creative vent widens. For this is where style is born in both writing and art, for art is the way you do a thing and an education based on art at once flashes out style.

The word "jalopy" made its fascinating appearance the other day. Brian wrote, "I went to town. I came back on a jalopy bus." This word stirred us. The others cross-questioned him on the character of such a bus. It turned out to mean "rackety" and although the word was picked up at once nevertheless they still ask for it to go up on the spelling list. We haven't had "jalopy" for spelling lately, Brian says. He loves spelling it, which is what I mean when I say that the drive is the children's own. It's all so merciful on a teacher.

Inescapably war and peace wait in an infant room; wait and vie.
True the toy shops are full of guns, boys' hands hold tanks and war planes while the blackboards, clay boards and easels burst with war play. But I'm unalarmed. My concern is the rearing of the creative disposition, for creativity in this crèche of living where people can still be changed must in the end defy, if not defeat, the capacity for destruction. Every happening in the infant room is either creative or destructive; every drawing, every shaping, every sentence and every dance goes one way or the other. For, as Erich Fromm says, "life has an inner dynamism of its own; it tends to grow, to be expressed, to be lived. The amount of destructiveness in a child is proportionate to the amount to which the expansiveness of his life has been curtailed. Destructiveness is the outcome of the unlived life."

I believe in this as passionately as the artist in his brush and the roadman in his shovel. For every work, and first of all that of a teacher, must have its form, its design. And the design of my work is that creativity in this time of life when character can be influenced forever is the solution to the problem of war. To me it has the validity of a law of physics and all the unstatable, irrepressible emotion of beauty.

Holidays

I must get this off my mind before I indulge in anything else. I met Mrs. Cutter in town recently and as she passed me she looked into a shop window and she turned Mark's face away too so that he should not see me. What made it worse was that I had a Maori companion with me: anathema to Mrs. Cutter.

The first thing Mark did when he returned to school after the holidays was to wait for me on the step (I was late), and when I went in to sit down he stood by me and held both my hands for some time.

I made a Maori belt for my cream coat with which to dazzle Wellington last week. It was a red, cream and black rafter-pattern from Porourangi, the meeting house at Waiomatatini, the darling of Sir Apirana Ngata's heart and the most comprehensive and spectacular meeting house in New Zealand. Everyone could not help but notice the belt, which made it very hard to wear. But only a few recognized its import: part of the advent of the New Zealand native culture at last into the European. It pacified me that it should be recognized for what it was in the higher rungs of thinking. It was, indeed, more than noticed. It received an emotional ovation. Not in the streets of course. There it was only something unusual and of an untoward brightness and something unrelated to what one sees in the shop windows. But in the informed areas, behind closed doors, it was acknowledged for what it was. Part of the Mighty Birth. The blended culture.

But even apart from that, its import, they loved it for the looks of it; for itself without the weight of its responsibility. And how I needed all this support. I did. I did. It called on more courage to wear this belt than it has done to wear anything else. But something unnameable, something irresistible and coming from the center of me, forced me to wear this belt about Wellington. But the trial of doing so was balanced. By what? By stray Maori eyes finding it. That was a prize! The way the little Maori girl in Woolworth's served me! You should have seen her. I might have been her most desired warrior. The friend who was with me was quite fascinated. And a middle-aged Maori waitress just put down her plates and stopped in her tracks, and the way two young Maori men standing on the far corner suddenly decided to cross the street and pass me closely! Lambton Quay those spring mornings became a heady adventure.

Well, here I am at the end. I have had Tom in my room giving demonstration lessons in writing. They are excellent lessons and Colleen and I learn much.

My little white Dennis is in a nursing home with a nervous breakdown. Plunket* upbringing and a young ambitious mother bent on earning more and more money. She beats him with a stick. In my word experiments he told me he wasn't frightened of anything except the sky. But his mother said he was afraid even of the chickens. I have a burning desire to pick up some of my neurotic whites and keep them for a while. My white June (Plunket) is still on holiday, which I advised.

The traffic inspector was out here the other day wanting to know why our children rode their bikes across the foot-way of the large new bridge here and yet walked on the traffic way. There are many questions about our children that we can't answer.

Professor Baillie said the other day, "Tidiness kills education."
I said, "Say that again."
"Tidiness," he repeated for me, "kills education. I'm a very untidy person myself."
"We have no time to be tidy here. And all that material! The time it takes to find, and put away and look after! Give me a blackboard and chalk!"

---

* *Plunket:* a method of child rearing, successful physically but disastrous psychologically. Lord Plunket, Governor General of New Zealand about 1906, gave his name to this method.

So many teachers put the emphasis on appearance while the meaning is atrophied. I very seldom find good handwriting going with a good head. My perfect writers are excellent copyists. But my real creative, artistic brains are failures with a pencil. Look at Matawhero. Him I place among the brightest and most sensitive beings ever to pass my way.

I am disturbed, though, to see the pages of unrelated sentences in newcomers. Presumably sentences containing certain words in current learning. That's bad. Those are the first lessons in disintegration. Writing must be cohesive. An integrated, developing idea. Every word presented must be part of a grand design. A necessary part. Every morning after a period of free conversation my Little Ones, right down to the fives, write of something close to them. The words they use are words of *their* choosing and are necessary to them and are part of the developing idea in their young minds. There is *sequence* in what they write, and intense meaning, since each child writes about that thing that is on his mind. Otherwise it's all teacher. Education, fundamentally, is the increase of the percentage of the conscious in relation to the unconscious. It must be a developing idea. None of this is new, of course. It's the understood design of today's education.

Hearing singing on the spring air before dinner tonight, I looked down towards the pa. And there on the *roro** of the meeting house was the youth club practising for the contest tonight. It was good singing. And very different from the singing we got recently during the holidays when there was a hockey tournament down there. Beer singing. (And all this was over a loudspeaker from the pa hall with three amplifiers on top of the roof.) But even that was all right in its exuberant way. The first day and the first evening. Even the whole night through the next morning and the next evening, it was at least bearable. But it was the second night, right through, that it showed signs of deterioration (they forgot to turn off the loudspeaker on the roof). And after having had to listen to it all night until the second morning I couldn't see anything in it at all. Yet I took all that, believing in live and let live, right through that day and that night. But the *third* morning, being mere Pakehas, we had no more endurance left.

Hockey! What a joke! A mere excuse to get together. And by together, I mean just that. *Together.* All night and all day, in spirit and in body. A friend of mine attended two of these "hockey tournaments," but what I call "beer tournaments." They sing and drink all night. Till morning. Not that I don't know this. When we lived further from the Board we sang and drank just as well until morning on many an occasion, and these pa parties I have never seen equalled in any place and at

* *roro:* verandah.

any time of life. It's just that we didn't have three amplifiers on the roof.

Together. Maoris know all about fusion. The communal heart and the communal mind has not yet been wholly broken by the New Culture. I don't really quarrel with it. Beer and all. They might as well. One of the old drinking kuias said to me in Pipiriki, "I must have my happiness." I knew what she meant.

As for the police. They supply the beer! I'll stand by that. They do.

But every dark night has its star. I woke up one of these musical nights to a golden tenor through the clouds of sleep. It rose in height and volume until I was roused fully. It was Kahu. I opened my eyes. It was dawn. I closed them again. Kahu was not drunk. He was singing over the microphone down at the pa to what, by the sound, was a huge audience. This voice in the dawn was like a golden bird on the wing. Mounting, mounting *mounting!* It was some song I had not heard before. It rose to its climax and the end that is his own particular characteristic: a trill and a twist and last high note.

Its setting was a grand drunken debauch, but it is one of those moments that I'm going to count over again when I know death is near. Kahu in the dawn.

Now that the basketball is over we can pick up our orchestra again. The purpose of this is more social than musical. Understandably. Nevertheless a little music crept in. But more and better music will creep in this year. Everything has to begin somewhere. And this was a beginning.

When I teach people I marry them. I found this out last year when I began the orchestra. To do what I wanted them to do they had need to be like me. More than that. They had to be part of me. As the season progressed the lesson began to teach itself to me. I found that for good performances we had to be one thing. One organ. And physically they had to be near to each other and to me. We had to bundle into a heap round the piano. I say "we had to," but that's not it. They *did* pile up round me at the piano, irrespective of what I tried to make them do. However, I arranged their seating to face the audience and with a view to each child being visible; nevertheless, at the end of the song, there they would all be, married all over and round me.

Rules like the best sound coming from a throat or instrument when facing the auditorium were just walked over. Although I didn't learn that thing until I heard the . . . *saw* the youth club sing a lament at the tangi of Whareparita's twins. They were too shy to face the gathering, so instinctively, they turned inward into a ring, seeing only one another. As for me, I learnt this particular lesson once and for all. I know it now.

Now where was I? I was talking marriage with my orchestra. I would never have learnt this through any other medium but music, I'm sure. I've never learnt it all this time teaching. But now that I do know it I see it in other areas. There is quietly occurring in my infant room a grand espousal. To bring them to do what I want them to do they come near me, I draw them near me, in body and in spirit. They don't know it but I do. They become part of me, like a lover. The approach, little different. The askance observation first, the acceptance next, then the gradual or quick coming, until in the complete procuration, there glows the harmony, the peace.

And what is the birth? From the orchestra it is music, and from the infant room it is work. A long, perpetuating, never-ending, transmuting birth, beginning its labour every morning and a rest between pains every evening.

Now that I see this as espousal the prickly, difficult, obscured way clears. It's all so simple.

Tall words. Wild words. Grand words. But there is an even deeper meaning beneath it all. It's integration of my living. And integration of theirs.

All the rules of love-making apply to these spiritual and intellectual fusions. There must be only two, for instance. As soon as another allegiance pushes in, the first union breaks apart. Love interferes with fidelities. I can't teach in the true essential medium when that approaching face turns away to another interest. I have tried in the past to do this, before I knew what I know now, but the answer was grating, discord, and even hatred. When love turns away, now, I don't follow it. I sit and suffer, unprotesting, until I feel the tread of another step.

Thinking of these things I can see wonders in the past that I had not realized at the time. I remember how much time I spent *talking* to my A team. Endlessly through the cold winter I had them in my room, on the mat before me or sitting on the low desks, discussing, working things out, fine points, big issues, behaviour, clothes and manners on the field. I didn't know then what I was doing, that I was deep in a fertile espousal, not even when they played their way to the top of the province. But I do now. I do now.

Integration. That fatal, vital word continues to press upward before the inner eye. Married to the life about you. However small or however big the social horizon. For the environment at hand has little bearing on the expansion of the mind and spirit. "Accident of dwelling-place does not necessarily mean parochialism of the soul." The features of the countenance of Life are the same. There is jealousy, pity, envy, compassion, joy, death, industry and peace just the same. It's just as possible to live to the full in a narrow corner as it is in bigness. Irrelevantly Flaubert comes to mind. Maybe that is why he died in apoplexy too early. He wrote and created out and beyond his own small home town. But, you will answer, what about *Madame Bovary*? It was outside the intellectual horizon of Normandy. And think of the disintegration of writing *Salammbô*! Ah well . . .

I'm glad I know this at last, that to teach I need first to espouse. And in coming upon this at last I find myself in a not undesirable company. I remember André Gide: "When I am alone I feel that my life is slowing down, stopping, and that I am on the very verge of ceasing to exist. My heart beats only out of sympathy; I live only through others—by procuration, so to speak, and by espousals; and I never feel myself living so intensely as when I escape from myself to become no matter who."

In essence Yeats speaks the same conviction: writing to a fellow worker in the building of a new Ireland, "the test of one's harmony is one's power to absorb the heterogeneous and make it harmonious. Absorb Ireland and her tragedy and you will become the poet of a people, the poet of a new insurrection."

The word "marry" is interchangeable with his word "absorb."

As for Buber, the German, he speaks of teaching as the "pedagogical intercourse."

These men have their different characteristics of expression: but to me the core of thought is the same: I teach through espousal.

I've got so much to say that I'm going to stop trying to say it. This is the last lot of this diary. The level of it is rising over my head.

Its purpose has been already fulfilled. I was lonely, professionally. I wanted gifted, intimate understanding. I've had it. I'm no longer professionally lonely.

Before I stop I'll try to cover the very vital and organic pattern of my professional life over the last weeks. It's always when things happen that we have no time to record them. But I'll try to give the picture, the conglomeration of imagery that has been banking up before the inner eye, waiting and pushing for expression. And the order will be its own. An order of emotional importance.

Stronger than any other image in the world behind is one of Mr. Tremaine in my infant room last week saying to me softly, "I want to hear you speak." Through everything else I hear this. Right through the Ballet on Thursday evening, the evening of his visit, I heard this. True, he had brought with him Professor —— from the chair of —— and Dr. —— from the chair of —— at —— University College to meet me, but it was this modest sentence of Mr. Tremaine's that remains the strongest thought within. The strongest sensation.

He kept from me who the visitors were. They had come to see my Maori primer books. They got me talking, Mr. Tremaine did, and these two men I lectured from the infant-room table with all the fire of conviction I had in me on the results of my recent experiments with the Key Vocabulary. I'm not going into these findings here since they are all presented in my Maori Infant Reading Scheme which is now looking for a publisher.

"The way," I reproved Mr. Tremaine at morning tea in the ugly old porch, "you come out here and make me talk. You make me talk! I talk everyone down for an hour, then feel ashamed of it afterwards!"

He smiled in enjoyment. "I always find," he told us, "that if I keep quiet I learn something."

"Are you important?" I asked the visitors.

"Oh no, no!"

"Well, as long as I know. I would have passed you your tea first. Anyway Mr. Tremaine, I like your technique of dropping important people on us. If I knew they were coming I'd never be here!"

He roared at this and I wondered what for. Some secret interpretation he had. But as he shook my hand goodbye in the porch I said, "I'm attacking Maori delinquency."

"Thank you for all the work you are doing," he replied. "And I enjoyed listening to you."

That was the day I gave him my Maori Infant Reading Scheme. He stood in the cold outside, so very big and tall in his greatcoat, turning over the pages, and dwelling on de Maupassant's lovely thought. He put his finger on the schematic drawings of Ihaka with which I had introduced it. "Look at this," he said tenderly. Ah, the simple rapture of fulfilment at my work being understood that cold morning. What unutterable reward for my labour.

JAMES HERNDON

The Price of Amphibians

An expression only has meaning within the stream of life.
— WITTGENSTEIN

This chapter is about the fact that it is so, that an expression only has meaning within the stream of life. It is also about the logical notion that in order, roughly, to know what something is (within the stream of life) you ought to be able to know what would be the case if it were not.

Alienation is such an expression. Within that particular tributary which is a school, it has the meaning that an individual gives up his Self (denying what he knows to be so in favor of what the school says is so) in order to achieve success and avoid failure. Of course, success and failure are expressions too and only have meaning within the stream in question, but by the time anyone remembers that, he is usually forty and reduced to writing about it.

For my students, and for myself, this alienation from ourselves means in practice that they (we) do or don't do things as a matter of reaction—as if we came in to school each day as so many blanks, having wiped ourselves clean of desire between breakfast and getting off the bus or out of our car. We turn ourselves off as I turn off the car radio just when the front wheels hit the curb at the teachers' parking lot. Once officially in the school we dispose of our cans of Coke and our smokes and await the presentation of our daily (streams of) lives by the school, and it is to that presentation that we respond. Re-act. We don't act first ourselves, and let the school respond (while we watch it), for the reason that we are alienated (as presupposed) and because we are sane.

From *How to Survive in Your Native Land* by James Herndon. Copyright © 1971 by James Herndon. Reprinted by permission of Simon & Schuster, Inc., and the author.

What would we be like (what would be the case) if we were not? Not alienated. From ourSelves.

In September of 1967 I looked through the cumulative folders of the kids we were going to have at Rabbit Mountain for the coming year, that is to say, the next Monday. I read what I already knew—the first grader with testable high IQ, the remarked bright student, leader, reads-at-third-grade-level, headed for the big time; and the fourth grader with low-average capability, IQ 89, lazy kid, must-be-pushed-to-achieve, reads-at-second-grade-level, discipline-problem, parents cooperative. The first grader and the fourth grader are the same kid.

I was not prepared for the phrase *identifies with amphibians*. The rest of the remarks on this kid's folder were indefinite. It was as if the folder was composed entirely of question marks. *Lazy, bright, success, leader, follower, reading level, achievement, cooperation,* apparently didn't come into it, so the teachers wrote what amounted to nothing. Only the one teacher, having written out (I imagined) some thirty such folders before, bored and maddened by the effort, had torn this one remark out of the systematic abstraction of the school's nature. It was as if, in the middle of the seventh grade social studies book about the amount of flax cultivated by Palestinian Arabs in their refugee camps, I could come across a page from *The Golden Bough* or an engraving of a priapus.

Monday mornings on the first day of school all kids come in and sit down to await announcement by the teacher of their daily lives in that class, that period. It is surprising how beautiful they are, even as blanks —or as they wait, filling in the blanks with future re-actions as you talk —and all the teachers every first day are full of enthusiasm and even hope, as if they finally had gotten a Good Class and now, they seem to say, Watch me teach! Richard didn't come in and sit down and await anything. He came in the door and straight up to me, smiling and holding an eight-inch brown-backed yellow-bellied water dog out to me in his right hand, saying Did you ever see a water dog before?

A water dog is a kind of newt or salamander common to all warm-water California coastal streams. I used to catch them all the time. Its skin is sandpapery. Perhaps it gets its name from the fact that its visage seems not to be reptilian but gives an odd impression of warm-bloodedness— you get the notion, if you hold a water dog, that it likes you. If you go underwater in streams like the Navarro you'll see them in deep holes, legs outspread, sinking slowly towards the bottom from which, when they reach it, they will push off and swim upwards, orange-bellied, towards the surface. They are amphibians.

Richard was a medium-sized twelve-year-old boy with a pleasant face, a wide smile, a blue jacket zipped up all the way. After showing me the water dog and telling me where he got it, he went back to the cabinets and began looking around for something to put the water dog in. While I called the roll and mispronounced names he found one of the aquariums and ran some water in it and put the water dog in it and while I talked about the school and its formalities he went outside and came back in with some rocks and some dirt for the aquarium and then he watched the water dog swim and crawl around. He took it out a couple of times and held it, but he didn't do any landscaping on the dirt and rocks because he knew the water dog didn't give a damn about that, and he didn't give a damn about that. He didn't make any noise and didn't disturb anyone, but all of us felt how utterly wrong his entire behavior was, since I was there in front of the class talking and they were sitting down pretending to listen and he was wandering around inside and outside with dirt and rocks and fooling with the water dog and all of us wanted to do it too and so we knew it was wrong. He didn't seem to be listening to what I was saying but when I got to the part where I explained that if you were absent you had to bring a note the next day, or if you were leaving school to go to the dentist or something you had to bring a note and give it to the health office, Richard raised his hand. What about, he asked, if you were going to your psychiatrist? Well. That told us all we wanted to know. The water dog, roaming around, that dirt, wandering in and out, not sitting down—things all the kids would be doing or wanting to do all the time, but which no one would do on the first day. We were dealing with a nut. That made it easy to understand.

I've always wondered what made Richard ask that. He never again referred to any psychiatrist or to therapy or anything of the sort. Perhaps he really wanted to know if the procedure was the same. I don't know.

For the first weeks of that year, Richard got along very badly. Everything he did seemed to be odd and not with it—everything he did got to be the focus of everyone's resentment and terror in the first few weeks of What To Do? In a very direct way he was ruining me as the teacher, or in the way I was trying to work with the kids as their teacher. That is, the kids attacked him precisely where I couldn't stand it, as if they (the other kids and Richard) had conspired to involve my personal terrors from the start. The kids attacked the water dog, they attacked Richard, and they revenged themselves on the thin black blind worm-salamanders which he brought into the aquarium, dive-bombing them with rocks, putting them on the heater, throwing them against the wall.

They attacked things he made. We had a big box of wood scraps from the shop and of beautiful odds and ends from a picture-framing shop and everyone was gluing them together with white glue and making constructions. But whereas everyone else made abstract architectural monuments (having already been to school art classes where any image of the real had been forbidden for some years) Richard preferred to make little toy trains and streetcars and tracks for them and then he played with them. He didn't play with them for long though, for the kids smashed them almost as quickly as he made them, threw them, stomped them, broke them, laughing and with anger.

Richard reacted to these acts with squeals of rage, with tears, with demands to me. He made placards from construction paper on which he wrote appeals to public opinion and to authority in the form of the vice-principal:

> Some kids in the eighth grade, like [followed by a list of names] are wrecking trains made by Richard S. All people in the school must get together and beat them up so they can never do it again.
>
> To the V.P.! Cruelty to animals is against nature. These kids are killing salamanders by heat and by bombing with rocks. They are [list of names]. Call them into the office and suspend them for ten days.

He taped these placards up on the walls of the room, he put them up in the halls outside, he hung them in the office, he even took them into the V.P.'s office and put them on his desk. The placards drove the other kids wild. They couldn't stand to see their names up there in public association with cruel arts, and they were really afraid that the V.P. *would* call them in, *would* suspend them, *would* call their mothers (it was the beginning, I can see now, of Richard's magical power) and so they tore the placards down, they threatened Richard, they hit him, killed the water dog, approached me with demands.

In the middle of all that, Richard displayed another eccentricity which provided excuse for revenge—namely, he had a great love for a kind of small-time obscenity. It mainly revolved around the word *dick*. (He never said any of the other common kid swear words; he said fucking, but never fuck, and he only used it to mean actual intercourse, never as just another vulgarity.)

So anyway, my memory has an image of Richard in an ebullient mood, having forgotten for the moment about cruelty, going around to kids talking about their dicks, and inevitably being persuaded by boys to go up to the girls and say something dirty. What Richard usually said was *Take out your dick!* The girls, the very same girls who were saying all the words Richard didn't say all the time and writing Fuck and Fuck you and Let's fuck in lipstick on the walls of the girls' bathroom, reacted with indignation and slapped Richard and made demands of me. When I foolishly told them to forget it, they counterattacked by going to see the V.P. and telling him (with what mixture of sexuality and prudishness can be imagined) about Richard told them to take out their dicks, and so he called in Richard and talked to him warily about dicks and girls and forbade Richard to say dick . . . and of course this counterattack enabled him to totally ignore Richard's own public complaints about kids who tortured amphibians to death and broke things you made, for somehow that didn't count alongside some nut or freak kid who told girls to take out their dicks! That was something you could get involved with! That you could take seriously! But dead salamanders, well . . .

(See man, this is what an American public school *is*. Let's cut out talking that shit about curriculum and learning about flax and all. The above is a School. Get it through your heads.)

All of this put me in the middle. I had to get mad at the kids who bombed the salamanders. I had to get mad at the kids who broke Richard's stuff. I had to discuss the phony outrage about dicks. I had to hear from the V.P. about should Richard be in EH class. The worst thing was that my anger was real. I felt capable of killing a kid who stood there laughing while a moist salamander fried on the heater. I did hate the chickenshit girls. And I also began to hate Richard for his utter childishness, his ignorance of what the other kids were up to, his failure to respond as a twelve-year-old ought, his total remoteness from group custom and behavior. For, instead of staying neutral (which was my plan) while the kids sweated out the crucial problem of Who Are We In This Room and What Shall We Do, I was being forced into the position of forbidding stuff all the time, of threatening, of being angry, or moralizing. It didn't matter, somehow, that it was real—that is, I really did think the killing and breaking was wrong. It didn't matter that I really thought everyone should be able to tolerate Richard. And it especially didn't matter that what I was really furious about was true—that they were attacking Richard as a substitute, as an excuse for not attacking those things which were at the root of their anxiety and frenzy, but which involved some risk in attacking, namely their parents and teachers and their lives at school eight hours a day.

So it was really quite nutty. On the one hand, I kept wishing Richard would start building abstract junk, call people assholes when he thought I wasn't listening (or deny it if I heard it), pitch pennies against the wall, smoke in the bathroom, break other kids' stuff or throw chalk, torture the water dog, make hip teen-age sexual innuendo to the girls, complain about mean teachers and grades and that he wasn't learning anything, and speak sagely of marijuana, using the words *pot* and *lid* a lot . . . in fact, become just like the other kids. Then I could *work with him, straighten him out,* get him to face his *real situation*—in short, do what I was ready to do, what the class was for, what I figured to do with the group. What was that? Why, merely to force them, through my existence in the room as *person* rather than giver of daily streams of life against which to react, rather than as successful or unsuccessful entertainer, to decide the course of their own lives.

On the other hand, that goddamn Richard was already at the point I hoped the other kids would reach. He already knew what he wanted to do, every moment of the day, he was prepared to do it, and could do it, did do it, liked to do it, it harmed no one, it wasn't isolated from his total life (he continued at school the things he did at home), he used the school's resources (science books, films, maps, geographics, aquarium, dirt and rocks)—he knew what he wanted, learned from it, required no instruction, shared his knowledge and experience, asked advice . . . he was there! It was great! It was also intolerable, because he was nuts. No one planned to put up with a nut who was also content. He wasn't alienated. No one could stand it. He was fair game.

Then changes began to happen. Richard made some of them. He stopped building trains and stuff. He didn't bring any more salamanders or water dogs. He began to concentrate on drawing cartoons and drawing maps. He made the cartoons on ordinary school paper, and the maps on huge pieces of butcher paper which he got from the office. They had a weird kind of association. The maps covered eight-foot-long pieces of paper with streets, freeways, alleys, telephone poles, street signs, street lights, bridges, underpasses, streetcar lines, depots, bus stations, bus stops, train stations and airports. The main characters in the cartoons were automobiles—generally old, famous makes like Duesenberg and Rolls ("Hey, Duse," a Rolls would ask, "What happened to you?")—and talking fireplugs and talking telephone poles and talking buildings, plus an occasional human who was usually identified as one of the members of the class or as myself and who had a bit part. Events in the classroom always played a role—someone who had attacked Richard found himself being run over by a Duesenberg somewhere in the cartoon, for instance, and when a lot of kids began to play chess later on, talking chesspieces began to enter into the action.

In itself, this changed nothing. The cartoons and maps only emphasized what everyone knew—that Richard was a nut and a babyish nut to boot. He kept wanting to show them to everyone and everyone kept being disgusted and upset. His writing, for one thing, was quite illegible; it was too large, too crowded, didn't go in a straight line. (The school nurse, confronted with some of it, wanted to talk about brain damage.) He writes like a baby! everyone wanted to say. That didn't matter to Richard, since he wanted to read it out loud to everyone anyway. (Looked at from this standpoint, it was rather literate, involved somewhat sophisticated puns and was at least as interesting as the average comic book.)

The change had more to do with Tizzo and Junior and Karl, who were the Big Three of the class, and who had a certain identity in the school as a Big Three. It's odd how these combinations occur among kids. The three were in no way alike and there seemed no objective reason for either their association or their identification as a unit. Perhaps it was a question of superlatives. Tizzo, for instance, was the toughest kid in school, with the possible exception of one other boy. (All year long kids tried to instigate a fight between the two, but it never happened.) Karl was the hippest kid in school, in the superficial sense of hipness which prevails among twelve- and thirteen-year-olds. He had the longest hair, knew all the music, associated with musicians (but did not play) and was one of the few kids (at that time) who actually smoked, rather than just talked about, grass. Junior could only be called the charming-est, or perhaps the carefree-est. He was beautiful, for one thing—dark curly hair, an open, friendly face, smiling, unworried, not angry, expressive of some term like happy-go-lucky.

In their relations to the school, they were equally diverse. Tizzo was a kid from an earlier age and another place. He didn't criticize the existence of the school, didn't question the rightness of its principles, didn't object to his place in it, which was to get (as he saw it) average grades (not too many D's and F's) and stay out of trouble. His trouble was his great anger at injustices within the system, as they affected him. He took it for granted that teachers were mean (else how would they control guys like him?) but there were limits. If a teacher didn't let him out of class every day to go to the bathroom (and have a smoke) that was reasonable; if the teacher never let him out, or gave him moral lectures when he asked, that was unreasonable. If he didn't try in a class and got an F or a D, that was O.K. if he *tried* (at least sometimes) and still got an F or D, that was unreasonable. When it was unreasonable, he got angry, slammed books, cursed the teacher, hit other kids, and got in trouble.

Karl was a critic. His aim was to get out of school as soon as possible. He wasn't concerned about degrees of things. He resented being made to go to class and was uninterested in whether the teacher was good or bad, nice or mean. His goal was the Continuation School, where his older brother had gone and where all the hip kids went (according to Karl), where they let you smoke in class, and where you could learn what's happening. He constantly criticized the structure of the school and the curriculum. His grounds for discontent were that it was useless and irrelevant. His philosophy was direct and simple, and also typical; he did nothing to hurt anyone else, therefore he should be allowed to do as he pleased. It was his business; he had nothing to learn from anyone.

Tizzo and Karl, however, both attended regularly, Tizzo in order to keep out of trouble and stick to his Roman sense of order, and Karl because only at school could you get a sizable audience for existential criticism of it. Junior, by contrast, came when he felt like it, almost always late, sometimes not at all. My image of Junior is of him coming in the room at eleven and saying that he thought he'd drop by for lunch. When he dropped in, he was immediately the center of attention. What did you do all morning? everyone would ask. Well, Junior hadn't done anything. I just watched Captain Kangaroo, he'd say smiling, and then I went back to sleep and got up and ate some stuff and got dressed and thought I'd come on over here for lunch. Hey, Mr. Herndon, he'd say, can I go out to the bathroom? And then Junior and five or six other lucky kids would go over to the bathroom and smoke and talk until lunchtime. I always felt good when Junior wandered in, and so I knew the kids felt it also. It was good to have him around (that's all you can say), you missed him when he wasn't there, and that was his superlative quality.

I want to remark here about fathers, or upon the absence of them. Unlike black inner-city ghetto poor deprived (choose your term) schools, most kids officially had fathers in our district, but in fact fathers were rarely mentioned. Kids talked about mothers. It was mothers they tried to satisfy, mothers who got mad if you got in trouble, mothers who came (with few exceptions) to the school, mothers who wanted you to get good grades and go to college, mothers who wrote you fake excuses (like Junior) or who you didn't want to feel ashamed of you (like Karl). I think I can tell a kid who has a real relationship with his father within a week of having him in class, it is that unusual. The point, for the present story, is that Tizzo was such a kid. He had an Italian father. His father was (according to Tizzo) rough and tough and would beat the hell out of him if he got in trouble. He wanted to avoid it. His father thought he ought to go to school, be clean and neat, get there on time, not smart off to the teachers, and not flunk. Period. Tizzo had a lot of tales about how strong his father was, even though he was smaller than Tizzo, who was at thirteen already a man physically, being about five feet ten and weighing perhaps a hundred and seventy. He also had a lot of tales about working with his father, going around with his father, fixing up the house with his father—in short, of manly relations with his father. In fact, he was learning how to be a father himself. He knew what his father did at work, what he did at home, what he thought, and how to please him. His concern was uncritical. His father was right, his demands not impossible; he Tizzo was imperfect and couldn't always control his temper and when he couldn't, deserved to be punished, deserved his father's anger, deserved to have to stay home instead of spending the day fishing for striped bass off the beaches of San Francisco. He didn't like the punishments, he thought the school could let up on him a bit and didn't have to be quite so tight, and he hoped continually for a break, a little luck in getting through, but he didn't criticize its general right to exist.

So the Three approached me one day. All of a sudden they were concerned about Richard. All these other little punks keep picking on him, they told me, and they had decided to do something about it. Richard has a right to exist even if he is nuts. He isn't hurting anyone else, said Karl, and so he has a right to do his thing. And everyone picks on him just because they are chickenshit, said Junior. They pick on him because he can't take up for himself, and because Richard is so nutty that the vice-principal won't do anything to them when they bug Richard, cause he thinks it's all Richard's fault because he is so crazy and tells the girls to take out their dicks. Tizzo said, They do it because they can get away with it!

So their analysis was that all kids would torment anyone and anything if they could get away with it. The only reason kids would act decently towards other creatures was if they were afraid of punishment for acting otherwise. That was what their lives, in and out of school, had taught them. They didn't treat Tizzo badly, because they were afraid he'd beat the shit out of them. They didn't treat Karl badly, because he'd put them down for being wimps and had the reputation to make it stick. They didn't treat Junior badly, because then he would smile at them and ask them to come along to the bathroom. Richard, having no saving graces of that kind, and having no protection from adults because he was nuts, had to take it.

Tizzo et al planned to turn things around. They proposed to supply the punishment to any kids who *bothered* Richard. Well, I said O.K. Why shouldn't I? It was a step in another, if not the right, direction. It also meant that Tizzo and Karl, who had been (to be honest) among Richard's chief persecutors, wouldn't be doing it any more, and that would be a break for Richard.

It became, immediately, an instrument of terror. All the kids became fair game themselves; they were in the same relationship to Tizzo and Karl and Junior as Richard had been to them. As soon as they had conferred with me, the Three foraged out firing on kids. They belted them for what they'd done a week ago to Richard, for what they'd told the V.P. a couple of days ago, for what they were planning on doing to Richard tomorrow. The three were full of anger. They hit half the kids and threatened the rest. If kids who were physically (if not morally) tougher than Karl or Junior protested, they were confronted with Tizzo. Girls, who were not to be hit according to Tizzo, were made to sit down in desks and not move. (If they moved, they were hit anyway. It was their own fault; they were told to stay put.)

We spent perhaps a week under the Terror, a week of outcry and protest and attempted discussion. Why was I allowing goon squad rule?

Why are you tormenting Richard?

How come Tizzo et al, who had been tormenting Richard, were all of a sudden allowed to hit kids for tormenting Richard?

How come you are all tormenting Richard?

How come we have to have some nutty kid in our room?

How come you bomb water dogs?

How come Richard gets to tell us to take out our dicks?

How come you want to write Let's fuck! on the bathroom walls?

How come Richard has to make all that nutty stuff?

How come you care what he does?

How come Tizzo and Karl and Junior, who are part of us, i.e., our leaders to whom we look up, turn against us when all we are doing is exercising our normal white sane American middle-class, or almost middle-class, prerogative of tormenting anyone and anything that isn't clearly us and tormenting it *without any fear of retribution?* What other good reason could there be for remaining this normal white, etc., with all its load of fear, guilt and alienation, than daily assurance of this reward? Why, considering our own agreement that everything we want to do—everything from writing Fuck you to talking to each other in class—is wrong and deserves punishment, ought some kid to be doing whatever he wants and think it is O.K.?

After about a week, the Terror began to peter out. Junior, having come to school regularly and early in order to keep Ordnung, began to arrive at noon. Tizzo and Karl found their interest beginning to flag. Perhaps they had only wanted to re-establish their Big Threeness in concrete terms; having done so, they didn't figure to keep up this eternal slugging. They weren't cruel, only angry. Still, it worked, in a way. Prevented by the goon squad from pinning the sins of the world on Richard, the class began to look elsewhere for something to do.

In the meantime, Richard, left relatively alone, had not been idle. He began to exploit his three major aptitudes—natural history, maps and magic. Indeed, he began to gain grudging admirers. He scoured the library and came up with fantastic photos of snakes devouring other beasts, or magnified tarantulas' jaws, or piranhas, cobras, moccasins and other death-dealing reptiles. No one could resist them. Since Richard was the only kid willing, at that time, to do the work necessary to produce this fascinating material, everyone had to gather around him in order to look, everyone had to hear his stock of snake lore and no one could just snatch the book and run and look at it by himself because of the Terror.

It was the same with his maps. He had begun to make huge maps on fifteen-foot lengths of butcher paper. To his great pleasure and astonishment he discovered that the school could afford butcher paper, as much as you wanted, in whatever lengths you wanted, as often as you wanted. Life was good. He spread the paper out on our long table, the ends drooping over, and covered it with freeways, overpasses, bridges, streets, alleys, stop signs, turn offs, thoroughfares, bus stops, streetcar tracks, depots, and the rest. Up until this time, we had all figured it was fantasy; our judgment was variously that it was interesting or nutty or disgusting but, either way, predicated on the fact of fantasy. When it was discovered that it was not fantasy, it was like revelation. How that happened I'm not sure, but, in any case, I recall kids coming up to me and saying that goddamn Richard says his maps are real and what did I think of that? So for a while we all stood around interrogating Richard about maps. Sometimes he was eager to answer—to trace the beginnings of a freeway in South San Francisco and show where it went, where bus connections could be made, where turnoffs to Tierra Firma could be expected—but at other times he displayed irritation, an irritation directed at dilettantes who were (1) not serious and (2) *bothering* him by getting in the way of his work. Still, he was convincing. If a kid asked, Rich (all of a sudden it was Rich, not Richard-you-nut), how would you get from here to Haight-Ashbury (mentioning one of the few places in the city that all the kids had heard of), what bus would you take? then Richard would stop working and get serious and answer the question in detail; what jitney to take, where to get off, what number bus to get on then, what street to transfer at, where to get off and then walk two blocks north . . . or kids who had once lived in San Francisco would say, Look, Rich, I used to live at such and such a street, number so and so, tell me what bus goes by there and where it came from and where it goes. Richard would think a bit and then say, Well, it would be Muni bus Number 48 (or whatever) coming from . . . and then go ahead and trace the entire route of the bus, street by street, finally allowing the bus to go right past the kid's former house on its journey into the mysteries of the city.

Then Richard's maps, having the decisive quality of the real, began to attract co-workers. It turned out that Richard was not against having houses drawn in on streets, or Doggie Diners or movie theaters. So that one morning I was treated to the sight of a bunch of kids sitting by the table over Richard's map, eagerly drawing in Marin's Travel Agency, Holt's Conservatory, Kohl's Burlesque (20—girls—20), Grand's Nursery (Exotic Plants), Stroud's Orpheum and Foundation, Spino's Health Farm, Perry's Gym, and so on. Other kids rushed me with demands for pencils, pens, marking pens and crayons and I got in a little sarcasm about *students* being *prepared* for work but in the end, not being prepared with any such items myself, had to send to the office for them. For I too had plans for Richard's map, and spent some time later elbow to elbow with kids (Move over! I can't move over, I'm drawing right here! Well I got to have room to draw! Well, I have to have room too!) drawing in Herndon's French Restaurant, a medieval affair with towers and moat and an immense menu featuring Sole Margeury with Petits Pois, which (I admit) was much admired.

Thus did Richard triumph momentarily over us all, a triumph in which we were happy to acquiesce. Richard's (now our) map was completed in perhaps a week and was hung up on the wall and admired, not only by us but by counselors and administrators and art consultants and visiting firemen from San Francisco State. It had a Fillmore district with soul food and dance halls and it had a Chinatown with opium dens and curio shops and it had museums and movies and Aquatic Park with bongo drummers and naked-lady sunbathers and it had a Haight-Ashbury with poster shops and drug emporiums and it had suburbs with shopping centers and houses with the kid's names on them and police stations and a gigantic Juvenile Hall with guard towers and machine guns and a big sign out front which said Junior's Juvi.

All in all it was pleasant to come in and watch fifteen or so kids sitting along the table opposite space on the map, drawing and coloring and looking at one another's stuff. Naturally we had incidents. There were bad guys who wanted to write Fuck on the map, and there were objections to the tyranny and unfairness of Richard, who, acting as Planning

Board, allotted drawing space according to some design in his mind not readily apparent to the rest of us. There was also some outcry about Richard's naming of the streets (a job he allowed no one else to do) wherein inevitably some kids had major freeways named after them (Tizzo Memorial Parkway) and others were only allotted minor streets or even alleys. Still, the map was finished, with an awful decrepit falling-down tenement named after the vice-principal, located on a tiny alley of the same name which was carefully decorated with garbage cans, old whiskey bottles and refuse. Two days later Tizzo got mad at Richard because of the Memorial Parkway. Some brave kid had pointed out to him that *Memorial* meant that he, Tizzo, was dead. What the hell, Rich, I thought I was your friend, said Tizzo. Sure, Tizzo, said Richard, you are. But that map's in the future! It's all in the future.

I doubt that Tizzo was satisfied by that answer, but all he could do about it was to remember some kid who had written a passing Fuck on the end of the Parkway and threaten him a bit.

Richard was probably the only kid who was not completely satisfied by the map. I could see he liked the attention and the unaccustomed feeling of working with other kids on a project of his invention. At the same time, he made it clear that they *bothered* him. He had to keep watch over them so that they didn't encroach on space he had allotted for something else. He had to argue with them about details. He had to take them into account, and that was a *bother*. More important, I think, he had to compromise his idea of reality—the map was now clearly a fantasy, could only be a fantasy, at best something of the future. It *might* come true; that was as close to the real as Richard could make it.

I said magic. Free of persecution and momentarily full of power as Director of Map Activities, Richard indulged himself. Kids began to rush me with complaints in a new key. Tell that fucking Rich to stop turning me into a frog! Richard said I was turned into a fart! He said I am immobile!

It's true, ain't it? I remembered to answer slyly. It's true, you *are* a frog, a fart, you can't move! No it ain't, they said, of course it isn't. What are you worried about then? I would say. But they *were* worried. Richard had them in the old grip of the Logos, and they genuinely didn't want him to do it.

The ritual was simple, Richard would come up to kids, walking on his toes and grinning with secret delight as usual, and ask them Say Om. (Or Say X or antidisestablishmentarianism or Shazam.) The kids couldn't ever resist and so they'd say it. Then Richard would say, You are now a frog, or Now you don't exist. Then the kids would disprove it (they hoped) by running hollering to me. They were prevented from solving it more simply by the memory of the Terror.

I enjoyed this action quite a bit, but in the end I could see everyone was really quite bugged and I began to tell Richard to lay off. I expected it to be difficult. All of a sudden we were some nomadic tribe caught between Attila-the-Big-Three and Richard-the-shaman. We alienated folk were in danger. I called Richard over and began to explain why he had to stop turning everyone into frogs. But Richard just said, innocently and quite reasonably, After all, Mr. Herndon, it's only a joke!

It was as if that remark, turning us almost against our will away from our urge towards supernatural explanations of all our difficulties, loaning us sanity and the real, just as mothers soothe their children at bedtime by telling them that TV program, that Monster, Vampire, The Glob, Murderer, they aren't real, they are just stories, they are made up, just pretend . . . the kids still have nightmares, of course, since nightmares can't be done away with by applications of reason like wet compresses, but they can be recognized and talked about as nightmares, given a name apart from breakfast or play or sunshine . . . as if that remark turned us off to Richard, diffused our focus on him, and let us back into our own lives in the classroom. Most likely, of course, it wasn't that at all, there was no actual moment of turning away but only some gradual release, unclear as to its moments, from our obsession. But memory wants to pinpoint its feeling of history, so as to make art. (The Muses are the daughters of Memory.) We began to go our own ways, ways which only occasionally touched Richard's or his ours. Kids occasionally did some drawing on Richard's maps. I occasionally stapled his cartoons up on the board alongside other stuff. Richard occasionally gave informal lectures on the habits of amphibians. When a group of kids developed a flourishing business making ceramic chesspieces he joined them, but not as a co-businessman. He made his own clay chesspieces alongside them, using the same clay at the same time, but that was all. His knights looked like sea horses, his pawns like tiny fireplugs.

The year went on. Richard wasn't the only kid in the class. Maps were not the only projects. Salamander torturing wasn't the only barbarism. Richard's mother came to see us a couple of times. She reminded us all of Richard; she gave the impression of being too placid, perhaps a bit vague, not worried enough. Naturally we had to see her in contrast to the mothers we usually saw who were mad for success, were outraged or wept, wanted to settle and fix everything in their kids' lives in half-hour conferences on their way to afternoon league play at the bowling alley. She mainly hoped that he would make some friends. She was happy with our program without knowing or caring to know much about it since Richard told her the school didn't bother him. I got a few calls from Richard's therapist, who wanted to know how he was getting along. It became clear that the therapist saw Rich as a pretty hopeless case, i.e., that he was never going to be a "normal" kid, that the best that could be hoped for with all the therapy in the world was that he could keep out of an institution and perhaps hold some kind of job like the ones social workers invent for severely retarded adults. Later in the year I worked up courage enough (and believed it enough) to tell the therapist about Richard's real ability and, more important to him (for Richard's intelligence didn't seem to him to be the issue so much as what he could *do* with it), about his actual acquired knowledge of the real world in concrete terms of geography and science. I told him I thought that if Richard could get through the age of being a kid and a teenager without being physically or spiritually murdered, that he might emerge (to a startled society composed of the therapist and ex-classmates and aging teachers) as a perfectly reasonable thirty-year-old citizen, albeit a bit eccentric like many another citizen, working at some fairly unusual job, one which very few other people could do. The therapist seemed to like the idea and in fact we both got a little excited about it then and there. He seemed to have visions of museums and classifying salamanders. I thought about the post office, where I used to work, and the difficulty of memorizing mail-routing schemes, the contests in the coffee rooms among supervisors and old hands about where certain streets were, what they used to be called, what routes served them, and so on, and I conjured up Richard, the Grey Eminence of the P.O. in a dusty back office drawing charts and schemes, settling disputes and reading the archives. In fact, when I thought of the future of America in terms of science-fiction (the predictions of which I always believe), I rather thought that Richard was one of the few kids in the class who had any real chance of having a job, of having work to do that a machine couldn't do and wouldn't be doing. Richard and Junior, by the way, whose uncle was a bail-bondsman.

P.S. Because the rest I write about Richard appears here like a postscript. Of course it ain't a postscript to Richard, or to Tizzo or to Richard's dad, or in fact at all to anyone, really. Readers ought to beware of the trouble with books. Still later in the year Richard's mother came to see us again, and she was quite upset for the first time. Richard's dad was upset, that was the thing. There was this report which Richard was supposed to write for his music class (a kind of music appreciation which all kids in the seventh grade take at our school, twelve weeks) and which he was in fact writing. Well, I'd seen him writing it in class and heard about it from him. Naturally he was writing about all sorts of old instruments and drawing pictures of talking Sackbuts and Serpents and Viols d'Amore and coming up to me with his sly and expectant grin and wanting to know if I knew what this and that was? But he was also writing it at home, and one evening his father took a look at Richard's report and apparently it was just the last straw for the father—there it was all scribbly and you couldn't read lots of it and there were maps and streets interspersed with accounts of Theobald Boehm inventing the flute —so the father got really angry and decided to show Richard how reports ought to be written and they sat down and talked about headings and footnotes and theses and paragraphs and documentation and clarity and so when that was all done and Richard indicated yes he understood what the issue was, the father told Richard to get going and rewrite that report and he did. I felt the father understood about Richard's real ability and intelligence and knowledge and curiosity and couldn't stand it, as we all can't, that Richard wouldn't put this all to use in normal bright-kid fashion, earning normal bright-kid success and evaluation. Along with that, I could imagine the father hoping Richard would get busy and play a little ball, get in a little normal trouble for smoking in the bathroom or cutting class.

So Richard did, but in the end wasn't able to hold to it and finally produced his big music report, name up in the right-hand corner and a title and skip a space and start in with a paragraph about sackbuts and a drawing centered nicely on the page and some more writing and then *Misericordia!* sprawled across the page, as Richard's mind made some irresistible connections in Xanadu, marched a procession of talking fireplugs, of cartoon frames enclosing Duesenbergs lecturing a crowd of applauding sea horses or chesspieces about musical instruments—Oh man, give a thought to fathers at this moment!

What is a teacher's part in this whole thing? It is only to pay attention and give protection. The rest I was able to leave to Tizzo. Tizzo maintained his relationship to Richard; he insisted on remaining Richard's friend. He kept an eye out for him, instructed him on what to do or what not to do, and he played with him. They played a game in the room where Richard was a bad ill-tempered car, speeding and going through red lights and being a road hog, and Tizzo was a police car and afterwards a judge who sentenced Richard-the-car to jail and locked him up in the closet. Then he would extract promises from the bad car about being good and reforming and let him out, at which the bad car would immediately start speeding around the room and have to get arrested all over again. Richard thought he'd like to play this game every day, but Tizzo saw that was no good. He restricted Richard to one day a week, usually Friday, and only one period. Often other kids would get into the game too. Although most kids complained about Richard's childishness all week long, many of them in fact found such childishness very attractive. Since Tizzo was doing it, they often permit themselves to play.

Tizzo, who had a father, was practicing up to be a father. He had a good use for Richard. Richard had a good use for Tizzo too, since he was learning to be a kid. Unlike the therapist and myself and Richard's own father, Tizzo didn't want Richard to turn into some other person, but only to accept the human condition. I can still hear him telling Richard forthrightly that he wasn't really a car (I know it, Tizzo, Richard would say, it's only a game) and that he could only pretend to be a car on Fridays. *That's the only day you can be a car!* Or, *Rich, I thought you were going to stop telling people to take out their dicks! Oh, yeah,* Richard would say, *I was, but I forgot. Bullshit, Rich, you didn't forget,* Tizzo would say, *you just wanted to and went ahead and did it.* Sometimes Tizzo would try to explain to Richard why it was that he could call people assholes and it would be O.K., and once in a while he'd try to get Richard to call someone an asshole, just to try it out and see if he got any satisfaction out of it, but Richard didn't want to call anyone an asshole, couldn't see any reason for it, and couldn't understand what Tizzo was getting at. In the end, all Tizzo was trying to get Richard to see was that human beings had to accept the idea of being *bothered* once in a while—that was what it was about. That if you accepted that, then you also could revolt against being bothered *all* the time, and that was as free as you could be.

Occasionally Richard would get mad at the tyranny of Tizzo and produce a placard:

> Some person in the eighth grade who thinks he is tough is trying to be Julius Caesar and tell other people what to do. The whole eighth grade should get together and make him stop doing this.

Then Tizzo would get mad and say he didn't care what Richard did and if the vice-principal got him it was just tough shit and Richard would indulge himself and be a car on Monday or Tuesday. Then suddenly it would be over and I could tell when it was. The bell would ring and it would be time for Tizzo to go to Reading, which he was mad at because Eileen wouldn't let him go to the bathroom—the bell would ring and Tizzo would just stand there in the room and I'd say Get going, Tizzo, and he'd say Sorry, Mr. Herndon, I can't go to Reading, Rich just turned me into a frog! And whenever that happened, Tizzo and Richard and I and many another kid standing around would laugh like hell and I would bang Tizzo on the back as he went out and he would hit me in the ribs and Richard would skip out grinning with his arms raised up like a cheering section and we would all recognize for an instant the foolishness and absurdity of our ways through the world and feel the impact of the great, occasional and accidental joy which would be our only reward along these paths.